THE
VICTORY
LAP

JACK YERMAN
& His Incredible Journey to the Olympics & Beyond

Bruce Hamilton Yerman

Front Cover

Philadelphia Feb. 3, 1963 -"COULDN'T CARE LESS – Two-month-old Bruce Yerman howls his distress at posing in silver cup. His daddy, Lt. Jack Yerman, USA, won in breaking meet record for 600-yard run at the Inquirer Games track meeting in Philadelphia last night. Yerman, a 1960 Olympian making final fling on indoor circuit, clocked a 1:11.2 to break record of 1.11.9 set by Mell Whitefield of New York a decade ago." *(AP Photo)*

Back Cover

Rome, Italy Sept. 8, 1960 - "The winners of the Men's 4 x 400 meters Relay Race on the podium at the Summer Olympic Games in Rome after the award. In the center are the gold medal winning American team made up of Glenn Davis; Otis Davis; Jack Yerman and Earl Young. At left is the silver medal winning German team of Manfred Kinder; Joachim Reske; Johannes Kaiser; and Carl Kaufmann. On the right are the bronze medalists from the West Indies consisting of George Kerr; James Wedderburn; Keith Gardner; and Malcolm Spence." *(AP Photo)*

Back Cover

Jack Yerman's 1960 Gold Medal *(Maya Yerman Sanchez Photo)*

THE VICTORY LAP

Jack Yerman and His Incredible Journey to the Olympics and Beyond

Copyright © 2021, Bruce Hamilton Yerman

Print ISBN: 978-1-66781-2-786

eBook ISBN: 978-1-66781-2-793

In Memory of

SUPER MOM

1939–2014

JACK YERMAN

World Records

Mile Relay

1600-Meter Relay

Two-Mile Relay

Distance Medley Relay

European Sprint Medley Relay

Indoor 400-Meter Short Track

660-Yard Sprint (Unofficial)

U.S. National Championships

Indoor 600 Yard (Twice)

400 Meters Olympic Trial

Mile Relay

Major Events

First US-USSR Dual Meet, 1958

Rose Bowl, 1959

Olympic Gold Medal, 1600-Meter Relay, 1960

Pan American Games

Council International Military (CISM),

International Champion, 1961-1963

Germany-United States Indoor Meet, Berlin, 1965

Honors

All-American, Track and Field

All University of California Athlete, Junior Year

University of California Hall of Fame

Sacramento Area Sports Hall of Fame

Woodland Sports Hall of Fame

Outstanding Service — Paradise High School Athletic Hall of Fame

and

Claims He Made a Hook Shot

Over Wilt Chamberlain in a Pick-Up game…

A note from the author:

I grew up listening to my father's stories. He shared his lessons in quiet places, such as driving to a basketball game, working together in the yard, or holding family meetings. Occasionally, I accompanied him when he spoke to groups of young people.

I learned that champions are people who do well in the face of adversity. Winners are determined, rise above weakness, and work through the pain, and real-life champions may not be on a track or court. They work in quiet places, at home with families, in offices or classrooms, and in mosques, churches, and synagogues serving others or pushing brooms at night to support loved ones.

Becoming a champion begins with how we meet problems head-on. It is not always clear what talents we have. Still, if we work hard at school or on the job, if we strive to be a better family member and friend, if we give our all, and if we practice the piano (or anything else) when we would rather not — if we push ourselves, the skills we develop during the difficult moments will reappear when we need them. Each of us has unique gifts, things that we do well, and where we find our talents is where we will grow into true champions.

The lessons learned on Jack's journey are as relevant today as when they happened.

The book references source documents to substantiate events, and dialogue has been recreated based on author interviews, newspaper articles, and published special-interest stories.

CONTENTS

PROLOGUE

Is It True?

Hanna sat in front of her computer, her finger twisting through a brown curl that had escaped down her forehead. She sat remembering the U.S. History teacher she had met two years earlier, third period on the first day of school. She had watched him while he watched students crisscross the room to find a seat. She had noticed his bright blue eyes from behind the timeless horn-rimmed glasses that sat comfortably on his bald head, with a touch of gray hair above his ears. She wondered how long ago the friendly worry lines had become permanent across his forehead, and she liked his gentle smile peeking through a casual, almost scruffy, beard.

Hanna took her seat on the first row directly facing the teacher's desk. The face of the desk was painted with a red, white, and blue Superman exploding towards her, his fist pushing upward, the other tucked aerodynamically by his side. The superhero bore the teacher's glasses on the same round head. The numerous nicks and scratches on the work of art told Hanna that the student who had produced it had long since moved on.

Hanna remembered how Chico's warm summer days had blended into a mild California autumn. She had watched the leaves of the giant twisted oak outside the classroom yellow, dry, and fall away. Hanna was sixteen at the time, an exchange student from the Netherlands at Chico High School. Her English improved with each passing week. History was her favorite class. She anticipated each day's revelations. She sat captivated along with the other students listening to the teacher's stories as if he had been there breathing, smelling, seeing and touching what others only read about in books.

It had been two years since Hanna had returned to her home country. She sat pondering, "How could his stories be true?" How could this bulky, balding, bespectacled teacher be the younger, slimmer, taller witness of the history he shared? She had imagined someone more attractive in his stories. Had she fallen for the teacher's deception, a trick of a master performer who made her believe in things that were not quite true—like the Superman painted on his desk?Determined to put her frustration behind, Hannah leaned towards her computer, opened her E-mail and pounded a letter onto the monitor:

```
Date: Friday, October 2, 1998
From: Hanna
Subject: Are your stories true?

I was an exchange student in your American History
class. I don't know if you remember me, but anyway,
I have a question that often pops into my mind: Are
your stories true? You covered a lot of history,
and it has bothered me because the information
you gave cannot be found anywhere. It would mean
a lot if I knew whether a "Yerman-story" was made
up to make me pay attention; or were you actually
part of all these things? ¹
```

Hanna rested her hands on the keyboard for a moment before hitting *Send*. If the teacher had been honest with her, if his stories had been true, if he had been part of history, perhaps she too could be a force in her world as he had been in his. She read her E-mail again because if it were not true, it would all be forgotten.

Hanna wrinkled the fading freckles on her nose and hit *SEND*.

PART I

Your Time Will Come

CHAPTER 1

Wanting It

The more I coached the more I became convinced that the mind, the will, the determination, the mental approach to competition are of the utmost importance. Yes, perhaps even more than the improvements in form and technique.[2]

Coach Brutus Hamilton

When asked how long he trained for the Olympics, Jack will typically answer, "Three or four years." Many who ask are looking for a quick answer—a two-and-a-half-minute success story. Several years after the Olympics, Jack asked Mr. Bailey, his former high school basketball coach, why, of all his teammates, he ran faster, traveled the world, played in the Rose Bowl, and graduated from the University of California and Stanford when others who had more talent did not. The coach replied, "It was important to you. You wanted it more than the others."

"I wanted it?"

Jack remembered his junior year in high school when he sat daydreaming in class and doodling on his physics paper. He wrote in the upper corner, "Gold Medal, 1960 Olympics. 400 meters." Sitting behind him was Cummings, a cocky boy who peaked over Jack's shoulder.

"You're stupid!" he derided. "You'll never do that." Up to that point, Jack had never won a race, but something inside said, "*Your time will come.*"

Wanting it began in his childhood home on 122 Fourth Street, in Woodland, California. Jack was a year old in 1940. The average home value in California was $3,527,[3] and Mom and Gram had pooled their resources to purchase a small, one-bedroom home for $500. It once had been a chicken coop on a long-ago farm, and it took Irene ten years to pay off the mortgage. Mom slept in the twin bed during the day, and the boy, Jack, shared it with his sister at night, their heads pointing in opposite directions.

Jack's childhood home
122 Fourth Street Woodland, California
(Jack and Margo Yerman Collection)

Jack never heard the words I love you in his home. He did not know that other mothers cradled their children and read to them before bed. The sanctuary of a loving hand pulling blankets up around his ears and feeling a mother's gentle kiss on the forehead was unknown to Jack. Words trickled from her mouth like sparse gravel. She never attended a church social, she never chatted with other women about the rising cost of milk, and she never gossiped about a neighbor. She never made a friend.

Irene was a thin woman. Her graying black hair was always short, requiring little attention. Her work wardrobe boasted a pair of white nurse's uniforms, and she walked silently in her soft white hospital shoes. At home, she threw on a housedress patterned with tiny flowers that had long since faded from repeated hand washing in the galvanized steel tub.

Irene sat for hours at the kitchen table, her sad blue eyes framed behind cat-eye glasses that curved upward to a point, staring at an imaginary spot somewhere on the bare white wall, her lips pursed around a cigarette and her left fingers forever tainted from the two packs a day while her right hand wrapped around a cup of day-old, bitter black coffee. Her mouth was in constant motion with or without the cigarette. Her furrowed lips puckered up and down, moving in and out, muscles randomly chewing like a cow on its cud.

Irene's timeless routine continued. The same yellow taxi transported her to Woodland Hospital five days a week, year after year. She earned an extra ten cents an hour working nights to support her two children and her mother, Bertha Flamme, known as Gram. Whenever possible, Irene volunteered for extra shifts. The yellow taxi deposited her back home, smelling of the tobacco she smoked and the sick people she tended.

Irene Yerman
(Jack and Margo Yerman Collection)

Irene seldom spoke. When she did, her slow and deliberate speech communicated basic everyday essentials. "We need to pay the electric bill." "I'm working an extra shift tonight." "Jack needs a new shirt. His other is ripped."

Jack's world of few words collided with first grade. In September of 1944, he entered school. He watched the other children say RED when the teacher held up the flashcard of a fire truck. They all said YELLOW looking at the card with a happy sun. They all said BLUE when she pointed to the pond with the duck floating in the middle. Some of his classmates saw the A in APPLE and the B in BOY, and the Z in ZEBRA, but Jack had never been exposed to the alphabet or basic school words in his home.

When others did not help Jack, he heard a still, small, comforting voice that seemed to whisper in his ear. It was a warm and kind voice, a man's voice, which reassured him when things did not go well. This unseen comforting companion filled his mother's emotionally absent gaps, softly speaking, "*Don't worry, your time will come.*"

Jack and his sister, Kathy

(*Jack and Margo Yerman Collection*)

Irene was reared a Baptist but did not claim any religion. She accompanied Jack and Kathy to the Methodist church on Christmas and Easter Sunday because it was only a few blocks from home. On those special days, she sat next to Jack until the compelling need for nicotine forced her away from the sermon. The remaining Sundays, through the four seasons, Mom and Kathy, Jack's older sister by two years, remained home while he dressed in his cleanest clothes, pushed his blond curly hair into order, and ran four blocks to the church. The congregation welcomed the boy who came alone, recited the Bible stories, sang the songs, and helped the minister and Sunday school teachers for five years without missing a Sunday. Jack puffed out his chest to receive his achievement bars that were pinned to his perfect attendance medals.

Sitting at home, Irene read her Bible, underlining passages with a pencil—she marked Proverbs more than the other books.

A good name is to be chosen rather than great riches, and loving favour rather than silver or gold. (Proverbs 22:1, KJV)

Withdraw thy foot from thy neighbor's house; lest he be weary of thee, and so hate thee. (Proverbs 25:17, KJV)

When Jack was born on February 5, 1939, his father, Loyd with one L, sat behind the bars of the Butte County Jail—the family guesses it was a fight, or maybe he was drunk, or perhaps he owed someone money, or maybe it was everything. The hospital clerk in Oroville wrote "Common Laborer" on the birth certificate. Jack's father had been a sunbaked broncobuster who wandered from one Northern California ranch to another. Loyd was good with ropes. He was fast on a horse and could lasso with the best, circling the noose overhead and finding the stretched-out neck of a terrified colt or the hind legs of a bawling calf on a dead run. Gritty work, wicked four-legged beasts, lonely bruises, and broken bones found solace in his growing consumption of painkillers and cheap alcohol.

Irene divorced the man before the boy's second birthday. She only said that it was best for the children, and years later, she told Jack that his father had a hankering for prostitutes. In time, Jack learned that Loyd had molested Kathy when she was a small child. After years of living in a stupor of drugs and alcohol on the streets of Old Sacramento, Loyd walked into the County Hospital and died of a heart attack on the waiting room floor at the age of fifty-five.

Bronco Bustin' Loyd Yerman
(Jack and Margo Yerman Collection)

Gram fed and watered the children while Irene slept during the day. Gram was a cookie-jar-shaped woman with a bulbous nose caught between her blue eyes. She rolled up her long hair in a conventional bun on the back of her head and never wore anything fancier than a simple cotton house-dress. She caught rainwater in a barrel for washing. She cooked pancakes for breakfast and made peanut butter sandwiches for lunch. Dinner varied between cheap pork chops or liver and onions with canned vegetables and potatoes. When money was in short supply at month's end, the children ate milk and toast that Gram warmed on the stove. The children never had snacks. They roamed the neighborhood after meals, and the extent of Gram's discipline for the boy was simply to say to Irene, "You need to speak to your son."

At each summer's end, Jack's lopsided and torn black leather Oxfords could barely contain his growing feet, and his scuffed knees peeked through the lingering white threads of his fading jeans. While his mother slept, Gram walked Jack to town for a new pair of shoes and one new pair of dark blue shrink-to-fit Levi's and an expensive Pendleton shirt: his only new clothes for the year. J.C. Penney had a layaway plan where a little money down reserved the jeans and the shirt until Gram could pay in full. The Sacramento Valley's heavy heat beat down hard in August while store's ventilating swamp coolers pushed a refreshing breeze through the store. Gram pulled Jack past the col-orful displays of pearly-button shirts that seemed to wave at him in the gentle flow of cool air. They walked past the stacks of blue, gray, black, and brown pants. If Jack asked Gram for anything beyond the shopping assignment, she would later tell Irene to talk to the boy. "Clothes don't make the man," Irene would say, but the quiet, small, comforting voice would interrupt Jack's disappointment, and he would hear, *Your time will come.*

Jack inhaled the pleasing aroma of processed cotton while he and Gram waited for the clerk. Gram explained to the man that the boy needed new pants. The man pulled out his white tape and measured the boy's bony waist. "Twenty-six inches," said the man, so that is what Gram bought. He pulled the chosen size of pocket-riveted jeans, holding them up to Jack—Jack knew they would be too small but would stretch as they did last year. Gram paid the clerk twenty-five cents to hold the pants on a special shelf until she could come up with the full two dollars and a few cents.

The people of Woodland bought shoes at Emil's Family Store on Main Street. A middle-aged salesman with a broad smile and a gold tooth welcomed his customers and talked of the warm day. He sat Jack down and moved the sliders on the metal measuring device to the boy's toes and instep. "You know," the man said, "people spend three-fourths of the day in their shoes, so it's gotta be properly fitted for a boy like this to grow strong." The man disappeared for a moment before returning with the selected shoe. Jack slid his foot inside, and the man cinched the laces. Jack stood and walked across the floor to the Fluoroscope. The wooden shoe-fitting machine stood four feet tall. He stepped to the lower platform and inched his toes into the X-ray box. Three looking glasses, like metal binoculars, positioned near eye level, peered down into the machine. The man flipped the switch and looked into his scope. He turned a knob until the needle on the gauge was in the correct position and then asked Jack and Gram to look into their assigned scopes. The three bent over the machine; their faces pressed to the metal frames like scientists peering into microscopes. They examined a green, glowing fluorescent screen with ghostly images of Oxford shoes wrapped around Jack's wiggling skeleton toes. The man affirmed that the boy had plenty of room to grow. Gram testified to the wisdom of the machine and paid the man. The two left the store and walked to a nearby cobbler to ask him to tack durable metal taps to the leather heels to extend the life of the shoes.

When summer reached its end and school began, Jack pulled his belt tight around the thick new denim that hugged his midsection. He reached down and folded the dragging cuffs. His toes wiggled in the stiff Oxfords that waited for a growing boy to stretch. Jack ran to school, his metal taps clickety-clacking on the pavement.

Jack at 12 years
(Jack and Margo Yerman Collection)

Children in Jack's neighborhood played without toys. Each afternoon, young people of all sizes trickled out of their homes onto Fourth Street to play tag or football, to design obstacle courses, and to race. When it was time to pick teams, Jack stood waiting, looking like the inspiration for Mad Magazine's Alfred E. Newman. Jack's curly blond hair was cut short over his prominent ears, and his thick lips framed his slightly crooked teeth. Jack's skinny arms swung back and forth. His legs rocked side to side. He was the smallest and always the last picked for team play. Jack waited while the big-kid captains holding the football pointed to the neighborhood favorites, then the hopefuls, and finally the "scabs" to round out the teams. Jack imagined himself winning when he played. He ran his fastest, he jumped his highest, and he pushed himself to his childhood limits. He dreamed he was the finest on Fourth Street. *"Your time will come."*

The RCA radio advertised the wonder of Christmas each December. Boys asked mothers for new plastic airplanes, the exact models of the machines that brothers and uncles were flying over Germany and the Pacific, replacing the wood-carved replicas that only pretended to be real. Children could slip a paper reel into the Viewmaster and peek through its lenses into a three-dimensional world that took them to the faraway Eiffel Tower. When they flipped the lever, the disk rotated, and they found the misty Niagara Falls. A new disk transported viewers across the world to an African safari where they stood facing a pride of majestic lions.

Christmas at the Yerman home, however, was practical. Irene searched the tree lots each Christmas until she found a small white fir with thin branches. She turned the tree with its best side facing frontward for Kathy and Jack to hang the painted glass decorations that Gram had collected over the years. Irene wrapped a pair of socks, a shirt, and underwear for her children and placed them under the small tree. Sometimes, she wrapped a toy—two years in a row, Jack opened the same wooden plaything on Christmas morning, a wooden block with a hammer and six colorful pegs to pound from one side of a block to the other. Jack never played with the toy.

When Jack was ten, a strange gift appeared under the tree wrapped in the same green and gold paper as the socks and underwear, but this mysterious package boasted distorted bumps and peculiar twists and turns. It had a metal pipe like a plumber might use, exposed at one end. Jack knelt to examine the package. He picked it up. It was heavy. He eyed the tarnished pipe and looked down its core, hoping to find its secret. He could see only blackness. He squeezed the wrinkled paper. He felt the puzzling hard bumps and the contradictory spongy places. He smelled the mysterious package and sensed only the cool metallic odor of the plumber's pipe. Jack's anticipation grew.

"Mom, what is it?"

Irene sat smoking.

"Tell me!" pleaded Jack.

Irene blew smoke at the imaginary spot on the wall.

"Tell me, please."

She turned to her cigarette.

The week before Christmas seemed like a month that stretched into a year. No amount of prodding would get Irene to talk. The anticipated morning arrived. Jack hurried to the tree. His mother, sister, and Gram might have been there, but he saw only the package. Jack pulled on the excessive amount of tape and string holding the layered paper together. He loosened the metal pipe, pulled it out, examined it, and concluded it was merely a deception. He stretched the clinging tape, and a rock the size of an orange fell to the floor. It, too, was nothing. He tore the green and gold paper at its edges, advancing to the package's core. A spongy ball of holey socks rolled out. He pulled with his hands, elbows outward, and the paper gave way. A brown rubber Voit football fell to the floor and wobbled away! Jack's arms flew in the air, a happy squeal erupted, and he tackled the ball to the hardwood floor. He rose to his knees and then to his feet, sending a smile to his watching mother.

Mom looked back at her animated son; a smile hidden behind her pursed lips clutching the cigarette. She paused for a moment to say, "Now you can play."

Jack took his ball outside and found his best friend, Charles Foster, "Hey Chuck, I got a ball. Let's play catch!" They rushed to Irene's giant backyard. After a few overarm passes, Chuck decided to punt the ball. He held it in front of him, took a half step back, then forward, and swung his right foot upward. Chuck's foot connected squarely, sending the ball end over end, arching over the walnut tree towards the neighbor's yard. Jack ran with his head cocked upwards, watching the descending ball. He reached, but the football fell inches beyond his grasp. It bounced off the neighbor's barbed-wire fence and hissed the ominous odor of stale air. Jack held the limp ball in his hands and felt a lump of devastation in his throat. Chuck went home. Jack returned to the house, tears building and beginning to roll down his cheeks. He held the lifeless ball out to his mother.

"I think it can be fixed," she said. "Take it to Cranston's."

Jack walked into Cranston's Hardware, past the paint, past the garden tools, and past the T-squares to the man in the apron busy behind the counter. "Excuse me, Mister," he said, catching the man's attention. "My mom bought this football here." Jack told his story about Christmas, Charles Foster, the kick, and the fence. "Can you fix it?"

Jack was too young to understand that eight years earlier, in 1942, Japan had strategically invaded the Dutch Indies and Singapore to control the rubber fields and 95 percent of the world's rubber market. The shortage plunged the United States into a crisis. Each Sherman tank's treads required a half-ton of the precious rubber, and each warship had twenty thousand rubber parts.[4] Rubber had been a scarce commodity in the United States, so even after the war and with the development of synthetic rubber, fixing rubber toys had not been familiar to the people in Cranston's Hardware store.

The man took the ball, rolled it over in his hands, touched the tiny hole, and looked back to Jack, "Kid, the Voit salesman comes to the store every two weeks. I'll ask him if he can do anything for you." Jack handed the ball to the man.

The clock moved slowly for two weeks, but the news at Cranston's was good. The salesman had taken Jack's ball and said he would bring it back in a month. On the designated day, Jack sprinted to the hardware store. His Oxfords beat the up-tempo tap of a boy anticipating his second Christmas. Jack pushed the store's glass door aside and walked across the wooden floor to the man at the counter. "Oh, the football," said the smiling clerk, taking extra time to pretend not to remember where he had shelved the ball before pulling it from under the counter. Jack took the football, looked at it, and rotated it in his hands. He moved the ball closer to his face. It smelled like a new tire. Jack found a quarter-sized patch perfectly blended over the hole. "Thank you!" he said as he ran out the door and back home.

Jack stood in the middle of Fourth Street with the ball resting between his forearm and his hip, just like the bigger boys. A football held peculiar powers in the fraternity of boys. It elevated Jack in the social pecking order. He was a bird with a bright feather, a reason to be among the young roosters who collected in front of their homes on Fourth Street or at the Beamer Park Grammar School playground. Jack had a ball, and the boys would find him. He was now certain to play every afternoon.

"Jack, your time will come."

CHAPTER 2

Life's not Fair

I was worried about you because you seemed so depressed after the meet. No need for that; it was just one of those days when running was hard work for you. Every athlete has such experiences. The problem is to set one's teeth against these disappointments and carry on even more enthusiastically and determined for the races ahead. I know you will do this.[5]

Coach Brutus Hamilton

Jack's introduction to injustice began when he was a year old. Irene had moved her little family to Woodland, next door to the Huberts. The Huberts had arrived in California as part of the great Dust Bowl migration from the South during the 1930s. After years of poor farming practices and a seven-year drought that sapped moisture from Oklahoma, Missouri, Arkansas, and Texas, massive dust storms consumed any hopes of making a living off the land. April 14, 1935 would be recorded in infamy as Black Sunday. A massive four-hour storm hurled choking dust and turned day into night while people huddled inside any hole they could find. It destroyed a third of the nation's wheat crops. At about the same time, California advertised for farmworkers. By 1940, two-hundred-thousand people moved from the parched southern plains to golden California.

The Hubert family struggled to find food, water, shelter, and work, like so many immigrants in the Sacramento Valley. Farm laborers earned a dollar a day. Many landowners forced the Okies to pay twenty-five cents a day to rent a tarpaper shack with a dirt floor and no plumbing. Personal hygiene was a luxury and something the Huberts had learned to live without.

But the Huberts were fighters. They eventually worked their way to Woodland and settled on Fourth Street. Mr. Hubert built rickety rental cabins behind his house out of salvaged lumber, cardboard boxes, broken plywood, and tarpaper. He filled most with relatives, and the Huberts grew into a herd of kids and cousins.

Jack remembers peering over the back fence at thirteen-year-old Peggy's "garden wedding," a notable social highlight on Fourth Street. The Hubert's yard was entirely void of vegetation and exuded the bitter smell of garbage and hardened dog feces. Peggy soon had three little boys of her own. When one of the boys was two years old, Peggy's husband rolled the pickup truck down the driveway without looking and backed over the toddler's head. The little lad was never quite right from then on.

Jack remembers Hallie, Teddy, Restoria, Peggy, Calvin, and Cecil. They were all a part of his growing up, whether he wanted them to be or not. One of Jack's first memories was standing on the street with the Hubert boys throwing pop bottles at passing cars. The Huberts had other destructive skills—they stole anything and everything. They took the vegetables from Irene's garden, the clothes off her line, and Jack's few toys. They stole his prized armada of miniature boats that he had crafted from halved walnut shells, clay, and toothpicks.

Mama Hubert was a corpulent three hundred pounds of rolling thunder. Her children could do no wrong. In contrast, Mr. Hubert was a cornstalk and looked twenty years older than his wife. His lower lip bulged of chewing tobacco. He passed the day spitting the sordid brown juice on everything, including the dog.

Hubert discipline employed a worn leather razor strap with a metal hook on end. The leather strap was an inch wide and two feet long. It had once been used to sharpen a straight edge razor, but now its purpose was to beat Hubert children. Jack could hear screams for what seemed to be hours as they each received their father's whippings. This was when father was king, and Mr. Hubert imposed his imperial sentences as he wished.

Calvin grew angrier and more callous with each of his beatings. He was a mean and nasty kid who gained his family's respect and prestige by pounding on Jack. During the summer, the older neighborhood boys organized boxing matches, slipped gloves onto Jack's hands, and matched him against Calvin. Jack was small and certainly not much of a challenge. Calvin pounded on him to the pleasure of the cheering Huberts.

In the third grade, Calvin stepped in line in front of Jack at the drinking fountain. Jack tapped him on the shoulder, "You shouldn't cut." Calvin replied with a full-knuckle blast to the mouth and nose. Jack never had a chance to pull his hands from his sides. The teacher sent both to the principal's office.

Jack sat in a chair next to Calvin, blood staining the front of his only school shirt as he held a compress to his battered nose.

"Calvin. Say you're sorry to Jack," said the principal, "and don't ever do that again."

Calvin looked at Jack, "I'm sorry, and I will never hit you again," he said, his voice dripping with sarcasm.

Jack found friends in other places. The Hennigans lived in the poorest house on a poor street. It looked to Jack as if the peeling paint and random roof shingles held the frame of their one-bedroom home together. Like Jack, they had no father, but there was always something going on with twelve kids. The Hennigans specialized in torturing small animals. They tied the tails of stray cats together and hung the frightened felines over the clothesline to watch them squirm and claw. They sometimes tied firecrackers to the poor animals.

Freddy Hennigan was Jack's age and dragged his clubfoot behind him, and they became friends walking to Beamer Park Grammar School. Freddy did not like first grade's *readin'*, *writin'*, and *'rithmatic*, so he invited Jack to skip school. As soon as first recess started, Freddy headed for home, and Jack followed. The two first-graders ditched school for several weeks, but rather than going straight home, they traveled over fences, hid behind houses, and played in vacant lots over a route that covered ten blocks. They arrived home at about the same hour as if they had attended school.

The boys miscalculated their timing one day, and Aunt Gladys found Jack at home in his play clothes. "Why aren't you in school?" she asked.

"I've been playing with Freddy," Jack responded.

"Playing with Freddy," questioned Aunt Gladys, "during the day?"

"We leave after recess," explained Jack.

Aunt Gladys's eyebrows narrowed, "Are you telling me that you've been skipping school?"

"I think so…" whimpered Jack.

"You put your school clothes on, and we're going back right now!" she demanded.

Jack learned his lesson while Freddy continued to struggle. None of the Hennigans finished the sixth grade.

A few children in Woodland were fortunate to be invited to play in one of three swimming pools. One belonged to Dr. Nichols, another to the Cranstons, who owned the hardware store, and another to the Wrights, whose father managed the Spreckels Sugar Refinery. The Fourth Street kids rode their bikes in the three-digit valley heat and looked through the fences of rich kids splashing in the blue water and jumping off diving boards.

Learning to swim without a pool was a problem. Irene walked Jack to the Thompson Bus Company and stood him next to a red line on the wall. The line was necessary because the bus would take anyone who reached the mark to the university pool fifteen miles away in Davis. Anyone below the red line could not stand in the shallow end and might drown. Jack had visited the bus station for three years before his head hit the line. When Jack learned to swim, he took Mr. Thompson's bus forty miles to Madison, a little town in the country where a farmer had built a large pool. Jack could spend the whole day in the water for a dollar.

Back on Fourth Street, children played never-ending kick-the-can, football, capture-the-flag, hedge volleyball, and roller skating. Bermuda grass carpeted Jack's large backyard and became the Fourth Street field when needed. Down the street, the Zaragozas had a basketball hoop nailed to a tree. The Zaragoza brothers, twins Joe and Lollie, were the best at everything. Years later, they would be the stars of the high school basketball team.

The group played kill-ball in the street. Half the mob lined up at the picket fence on one side of the road and the other half at the hedge on the opposite side. When Joe or Lollie gave the signal, everyone ran to the football in the middle. If you got the ball, you advanced through the mayhem to the other team's fence. The other team jumped on you, pulled your hair, and cut you down at the knees while your teammates pulled the attackers off the pile. You never gave up the ball; it was a sign of honor! Even with the tackling, scratching, pulling, and pounding, the only serious injuries occurred when a player landed on Jimmy Henderson's water faucet.

This is where Jack learned to play ball.

Children followed World War II on the documentary newsreels that flickered from the movie house projector. A man's deep voice narrated the courage of American troops in the air, on land, and at sea. The Fourth Street gang reenacted battles using rubber-band guns for pistols. Each wooden pistol held four shots—one on each side of the weapon, another on the top, and one underneath the barrel, all glued or nailed in place with clothespin triggers. Loops cut from old inner tubes served as ammunition. Jack would run behind a tree, take a shot, dive behind a bush, and launch a dirt-clod grenade into the battle.

Jack's backyard and the Fourth Street Battalion with rubber band guns.
Jack's head is turned.

(Jack and Margo Yerman Collection)

Jack was six years old when World War II ended. Then, something even better happened on Fourth Street. Everyone's brother, cousin, or uncle returned home loaded with army surplus. Kids chased each other around with Japanese swords, bayonets, German Luger pistols, signal flags, walkie-talkies, dummy grenades, signal mirrors, canteens, belts, hats, and uniforms. The

Fourth Street Battalion, loaded with helmets, uniforms, and weapons, dug trenches and foxholes in Jack's backyard. The labor force grew, digging skills increased, and a new project was conceived. Thirty kids marched two blocks north to a vacant lot behind Darrel Hermley's house. The company of small soldiers, working in unison, moved tons of dirt. The ground gave way to tunnels and chambers. The regiment furnished the underground fort with furniture, electricity provided from extension cords, and carpets until someone's parents investigated and discovered a missing living-room lamp. Neighbors summoned the city engineer, who inspected the underground fortress and called a crew of men with a dirt mover to fill the hazard.

Jack's neighborhood boundaries expanded as he grew older. His friends included the Owens boys on the next block, David Harrison, who lived two blocks over, and Norman Halden, who lived three blocks away, where the Huberts never went.

The day of reckoning arrived when Jack was eleven years old. Calvin hopped over the hog-wire fencing separating the back yards and sneered, "Jack, you're in trouble!"

As Calvin swung, Jack moved aside, grabbed Calvin's arm, and pulled him to the grass. Jack maneuvered to the left and wrapped his legs around the bully's torso. Jack squeezed Calvin's midsection in a scissor lock, reaching up and grabbing the boy's neck in a hammerlock. Jack's strength from biking and neighborhood games flowed through his powerful legs, and he squeezed harder, like a python sucking the air out of its prey. Calvin struggled for a moment. Jack saw the panic in his eyes.

"I'll get my brother!" threatened Calvin.

Jack hung on, feeling beads of sweat collecting on his forehead.

"Let me go! You're hurting me!" cried Calvin. "Let me go!"

Jack had waited for this moment for a long time. He smelled victory and tightened his grip even more. After nearly twenty minutes of squeezing, Calvin had no more fight left. He whined like a wounded puppy. Jack let him go. He had beaten his nemesis.

CHAPTER 3

To Tell the Truth

"Yes, victory is great, but sometimes when it cannot be helped, defeat also is great," sang Walt Whitman. No victory is great when it is brought at the sacrifice of ideals; and no defeat is disgraceful as long as one does his best and follows the gleam of idealism.[6]

Coach Brutus Hamilton

Twice, Irene bought three bus tickets and boarded her two children with sack lunches for a forty-five-minute trip to Sacramento. Irene never explained why they took the trip, but it was exciting for Kathy and Jack to leave Woodland. The bus terminal was a block from the state's capital, where Jack and Kathy played on the green lawns while Irene sat on a park bench smoking. She watched her children throw acorns at blue jays and run after grey squirrels that darted from tree to tree. When the food was gone, the children followed their mother's silent lead. They folded their brown paper bags and walked back to the bus station for home.

Another family outing was to walk five blocks from home to the railroad tracks and watch the train chug through town. Jack's shoes crunched over the grey gravel on the rocky bed supporting the tracks. He breathed in the oily aroma of creosote that oozed from the railroad ties. The tracks vibrated when the iron mountains approached, their bellowing horns announcing their arrival. The trains passed by, rumbling only a few feet from where Jack stood. He could feel the pounding reverberations in his chest, and his heart beat with the clatter of steel on the tracks. He watched the magical diesel engines pull, their bitter fumes tickling his nose. His mother watched with him. She seemed comforted by the mechanical harmony of power and steel. Jack waved to the man on the train. He wondered where the brawny metal cars had been and where they would go. He would have asked his mother, but he knew she would not answer. Irene looked down the long twin rails at the last car shrinking away. She turned, and Kathy and Jack followed her home.

Jack's classmates talked of driving through tunnels cut through the giant sequoias that reached to the heavens as if to hold up the sky. They spoke of the deep blue water in Lake Tahoe. Jack wished to smell the fresh forests hugging the California coast, and he imagined screaming down the wooden roller coaster at the Santa Cruz Boardwalk. He wondered if the sand seeping between his toes at the beach would feel something like the spongy river silt near town.

Not traveling was hard on Kathy. She was pretty, blond, blue-eyed, and two-years older than Jack. He watched his sister grow to adolescence and from innocence to seeking acceptance from the popular kids in town. The schoolgirls boasted of plans to soak in the sun at the beach over the Easter holiday. "My mother is going to buy me a new bathing suit," preened one of the girls who stood a little sideways, her shoulders turned back towards the group and her back arched, pushing her budding breasts further than they needed to go.

"Are you getting a bikini?" beamed Kathy, hoping for an invitation to join them. "Our mothers are thinking about it. We're going shopping this weekend," said the girl while the others smiled around her. Kathy knew there would be no invitation, and even if there were, she did not have the money. When Easter Week arrived, Kathy spread a towel in the backyard. She massaged her reddening skin with sweet-smelling coconut oils and rotated from her back to her stomach, her white skin baking until she reached the perfect shade of bronze. That next week Kathy stood with the girls, her golden tan confirming fabricated stories of running in the sand, playing volleyball with the boys, drinking sodas, and cooling in the salty waves.

Jack was eager to expand his world and told his mother that he wanted a bike. Two weeks later, a man arrived at the house with a large, faded blue bike. Irene gave the man twenty-five dollars, but the eight-year-old boy could not reach the pedals. It sat parked against the backyard shed for a year. Irene saved her money from the extra shifts she worked, and this time walked her son downtown to Ferrington's Appliance Store. There sat a glistening red Schwinn Ballooner equipped with a tank on the crossbar and a lamp on the front fender—the bike looked like a car. He sat on the bike. "It fits," Jack announced, and Irene handed the clerk the money. Jack rode his new bike home.

The bike was heavy, so Jack removed the tank from the crossbar, disconnected the chrome fenders, detached the bell and removed the flags that dangled from the handlebars. Jack's world increased thirty square miles on his new wheels. He peddled to Cache Creek five miles away to swim or pumped his bike the other direction to the warmer slough water. Jack would slow to a stop when he approached a farmer's freshly plowed field. He smelled the new soil and surveyed the soft furrows of uprooted dirt that beckoned him to a race. Jack dismounted, jumped the small irrigation ditch, and sprinted; he lifted his knees, denying the plowed earth the pleasure of pulling him down. The innate thrill of pushing himself to his childhood limits was electric.

Jack sits on the Schwinn Ballooner
(Jack and Margo Yerman Collection)

Jack rode his bike to the Woodland Library, where his friend, the librarian, introduced him to Alexandre Dumas, the author of *The Three Musketeers*. Jack took the book home, secluded himself in his backyard shed, and read. He imagined himself with D'Artagnan fighting alongside his loyal friends. He wished to be as wise as Athos, as powerful as Porthos, as shrewd as Aramis. He returned to the library and found *The Count of Monte Cristo*, and read:

> *Those born to wealth, and who have the means of gratifying every wish…know not what is the real happiness of life, just as those who have been tossed on the stormy waters of the ocean on a few frail planks can alone realize the blessings of fair weather.*[7]

Jack's childhood resilience and the still small voice reminding him that his *time would come* compensated for his mother's emotional absence. One afternoon, Jack walked by his mother as she sat at the kitchen table smoking her cigarette. This time, she stopped him and burst out, "When you're 18, you're out of here!" She returned to her cigarette, and Jack thought, *okay*, and walked on. Eighteen was still a few years away.

Some weeks after Irene's decree, Aunt Edith, Loyd's older sister, brought her new husband from Nevada to visit. Jack bounced through the door to find Edith sitting at the kitchen table. She had dyed her graying hair red and was as bubbly as a young spring bride. She invited Jack to sit for a moment. She and the man looked at him and then back at each other as if they shared a secret.

"Jack, we want to talk to you," she said, her voice elevating a note. "You know, we're married, and we don't have any kids."

He looked at Edith and watched the grinning man sitting next to her.

"We are wondering if you would like to live with us and be our son." Edith had talked to Irene, who had told her, "If he wants to go, it's fine with me."

Jack was in junior high school and had just made the basketball team. "I like it here," Jack said as he slid to the edge of his chair, stood up, and hurried out the back door.

Jack liked Irene's sisters, who brought welcomed changes to his routine. Sometimes Aunt Gladys invited him to stay at her home in Yuba City for the weekend, or Aunt Faye took him to the family farm in Nicolaus. Jack visited the farm two weeks each summer and again for a short time in the fall. He welcomed the early mornings and the refreshing aroma of freshly cut alfalfa. He breathed the sweet scent of garden corn. The dust from the walnut tree tickled his nose, and he loved the fragrance of ripening peaches that turned gold in the California sun. Aunt Faye had bird dogs, horses, milk cows, and cats, and Jack played with his younger cousins Mike, Bill, Marti, and Bob. He especially liked working with Mike, who could drive the truck and fix anything—including his younger brother Bill, whom he had once disciplined by hitting him on the head with a ball-peen hammer while babysitting. Bill recuperated by staying close to Aunt Faye in the house.

Jack grew older and watched the boys in Woodland paint, polish, and tune their cars for cruising up and down Main Street on Friday and Saturday nights. Cars in the 1950s were the size of living rooms, with large sofa-like seats. A "buck" of gas could fill the tank for the night. Teenagers packed into sedans as the sun set, and they synchronized radios to the Sacramento DJ spinning vinyl records. Some kids smoked cigarettes, and everyone had a soda—the guys looked like James Dean and the girls like Natalie Wood.

Cars meant freedom, friends, and girls. Jack had mowed lawns, worked at the bakery, and cleaned a chicken farm, but he needed real cash to buy a car. The sophomore counselor called Jack to his office. The man looked up, adjusted his glasses, and said, "Leithold Drugs needs a clerk-delivery boy. The best part of this job is you get to drive the delivery truck." Leithold Drug Company had been founded in 1890 by J.V. Leithold and now was managed by his two grandsons. "You need to go to the store and talk to the owners, Bill and Bob, the Griffith brothers," instructed the counselor. "They sell every-thing from food, to hardware, to camping supplies, and liquor."

Jack sprinted down Main Street, ran past the Woodland Opera House, and paused in front of Leithold Drugs. He pushed down his curly blond hair, tucked in his plaid shirt, and walked through the doors. Jack passed by the soda fountain with its sparkling chrome spouts, where the soda jerk pulled levers to mix combinations of carbonated water, flavored syrups, and scoops of ice cream. The straws and long-handled soda spoons waited for the afterschool crowd that assembled to chat, laugh, and watch the alchemist brewing his magic.

The younger brother, Bob, welcomed Jack and invited him to sit on the red stool at the end of the chrome-trimmed bar. They chatted about the job and the work of delivering lunches to offices and medicines to homes. Bob asked, "I have an important question for you. We need someone this summer, but we also need someone after school and on weekends next fall. I need to know whether you will be playing football."

Jack looked at Mr. Griffith. He was a thin, handsome man with dark hair, kind eyes, and an easy smile. Jack wanted to work here— but didn't the man understand the importance of football in this town? Jack was in a quandary. He had been playing football almost every day since opening the strange package under the Christmas tree years ago. He wanted this job and the car, and if he said, *"No, I'm not playing football,"* he would be working and have the money for a vehicle by summer's end. Jack could then claim to have changed his mind.

Jack looked at the polished red, white, and silver soda fountain. His eyes ran back and forth across the rows of tidy shelves. He watched the pharmacist in his white coat separating powders and pills with something that looked like a knife. He looked at Mr. Griffith, who sat waiting for an answer.

Jack confessed, "I'll be playing football." He knew this was the end of the interview.

Griffith looked at the boy. His mouth lay in a flat line rather than the easy smile he wore a minute ago, "I'm sorry, son. I would have hired you, but we need someone who can work afternoons in the fall." Jack returned home, looking down at the passing lines on the sidewalk. He wondered whether he had made a mistake. "Should I have lied?"

Two weeks later, Jack received a phone call. It was Bob Griffith. The voice was energetic, and the words were urgent, "Jack, can you work tomorrow?"

"You mean — I have the job?"

"Yup."

"I'll be there today!" and he *ran* to the store.

After several weeks of sweeping, stocking shelves, and delivering goods, Jack asked Bob why the change of mind. Mr. Griffith explained, "We knew how much you wanted the job and understood that you could have lied about playing football. You, however, chose to tell the truth." Bob shifted a little in his chair and leaned forward, "We need good, honest people working here. We have drugs, liquor, and valuable items that are a temptation to someone who lacks integrity."

The Griffith brothers gave him all the summer hours he could work. The Griffiths had replaced the truck with a fuel-saving three-wheeled Cushman motor scooter, and Jack darted around Woodland like a superhero with his white pharmacy coat flying in the wind behind him. He delivered food, medicines, and the daily supply of alcohol to older women who met him at the door smelling like yesterday's bottle.

Bill approached Jack one evening with an unusual request. "Jack, could you stay and clean the store tonight?"

"Me? Sure."

The place was enormous! Jack pushed the mop between the shelves for nearly two hours. He hefted and hauled the galvanized bucket of dirty water to the large sink and poured the muck down the swirling drain. Between wiping sweat from his forehead, he wondered what had happened to the maintenance company that usually cleaned the store. Bill later shared that the Woodland Chamber of Commerce president held the cleaning contracts for leading businesses in town and had keys to many of the stores. The trusted president had been helping himself to anything he pleased. Woodland's police department searched the man's house and found radios, furniture, and kitchen appliances — thousands of dollars' worth of goods. The president was not arrested, no articles printed in the newspaper, and the news was not broadcast on the radio. A few of the merchants and the police chief had gone to the man's home one evening and warned, "You have twenty-four hours to leave Woodland." Jack remembered the two teenage daughters — one of them had dropped out of Yolo County's Sugar Queen competition when her father left town.

The summer days grew shorter and the afternoon shadows longer. It was time to return to school. The fragrance of freshly cut grass and the symmetry of the white powdery chalk dividing the gridiron set the stage for the town's talk of this year's football team. It was the season, and the Griffiths gave Jack evening hours after football practice.

Jack had earned a dollar an hour and saved every cent. Irene contributed an additional two hundred dollars, and Jack had the money to buy a car. He walked to the Chevrolet dealer in town. The salesman pointed him to a two-door '52 Chevy.

"How much?" asked Jack.

"It's $695, but I'll give it to you today for $650."

Jack looked at the car; he touched the rounded hood. He thumped the tire with his shoe. He sat in the driver's seat and adjusted the rear-view mirror. "I'll take it. But you have to show me how to drive," he said. Jack had never driven a car.

Jack slid over, and the salesman sat behind the wheel to demonstrate the *three-on-the-tree* column-mounted shifter. The salesman moved the handle behind the steering wheel in an H formation from first to second to third gear and then back across to reverse. The engine roared when he turned the key and pressed the gas pedal. The car was alive, and Jack's pulse quickened to match the motor's power. The salesman backed out and maneuvered the car through the lot, pointed it towards the street, turned off the ignition, and traded places with Jack.

This was Jack's car! Jack pushed on the brake with his foot and then found the clutch. He squeezed the smooth steering wheel in his hands and reached up to the chrome gearshift. He practiced moving his hand to first, then second, third, and back to neutral. Jack turned the key, and the car ignited. The rumbling under the hood felt good. He put his foot on the clutch, shifted into first, and the vehicle convulsed forward and jerked to a stop. The man told Jack he would figure it out, shook his hand, patted him on the back, and wished him luck. Jack proceeded down the road, sputtering the engine as the car bounced through the gears.

Over the next few weeks, Jack dismantled the car. He removed the chrome and "chopped the top" to make the windows smaller. He applied putty and sanded the corners to mold his ride to a smooth, rounded appearance. He added whitewall tires, full moon hubcaps, and skirts over the back wheels. Wires — curb feelers — stretched from the fenders to warn the driver of the road's edge. He added a suicide knob to the steering wheel, a ball-like attachment that turned the wheel. A driver had to be careful when the wheels snapped back into position, and the knob flew around, potentially fracturing the driver's hand.

The car needed straight pipes and a "glasspack." Glasspacks, sometimes called cherry bombs, were perforated exhaust pipes encased in a layer of insulation. A guy could drive by a girl's house, downshift, and send a reverberating message from the engine that he was out front. Jack did not have the money for the pricey modification, so he hammered holes in his muffler until he found a similar tone, but he soon discovered that exhaust seeped through the floorboards when the car sat idling. Jack kept his car moving to avoid this problem.

When all the modifications were in place, he painted the automobile an eye-grabbing metallic blue-black. It was iridescent from one angle, and straight on, it looked vampire black. Jack could ride with the best of Woodland. On the way to school, Jack would pick up his best friend, Phil Persson. Phil and Jack's friendship dated back to the playground at Beamer Grammar School.

Four years prior, Mr. Page, the middle school basketball coach, ripped Jack's shirt at the seventh-grade tryouts. The boys were running *the weave,* a drill where players pass the ball forward and run behind each other as they move across the imaginary lanes on the court. Jack had never seen the weave, and as soon as the ball hit his hands, he was bewildered, throwing it to the wrong person and running in the wrong direction. Mr. Page screamed at Jack, grabbed the boy by the shirt. Jack felt like a marionette under the coach's menacing grip and heard his Pendleton fabric tear down the back. The ripped shirt fluttered. Jack's eyes filled with tears, but he remained at practice. This was his only new shirt for the year.

A year later, it was Mr. Page who casually called out to Phil during recess, "Hey, you gotta come with me; your dad just died!" Phil froze in place — the basketball rolling away. "Come on, let's go," demanded Mr. Page. Phil's father had been crushed in a tractor rollover while working in the fields near Woodland. Jack's stomach tightened, and his heart hurt.

The boys' friendship grew. They played basketball until dark, ate together, applied the same hair goop, and dressed in blue jeans and t-shirts. They drove to the Santa Cruz Beach Boardwalk, Lake Tahoe's crystal blue waters, and 49er's football games. Phil was confident. He did not swear or drink beer, and Jack felt comfortable around him. Phil was religious and a Mormon.

Jack picked Phil up at his home on the way to school. Phil slipped onto the passenger seat of the two-door '52 Chevy. He had already attended his early morning seminary class at his church. Phil shifted his book bag in his lap, looked at Jack, and asked, "Do you think God talks to people?"

Jack thought for a moment, "What do you mean?"

You know, people like you and me," replied Phil. "Do you think that God talks to regular people, not just with holy men? Anyone can talk to God if they want to."

Jack and Phil in High School
(Jack and Margo Yerman Collection)

The idea that God talked to people felt familiar. When Jack was younger and the last chosen in neighborhood pickup-ball, or when the teacher at school assigned him to the lowest reading group, or when someone said, *you're stupid*, or *you're a loser*, Jack heard another voice, a voice that whispered inside of him. It was an unseen comforting companion that filled him with confidence. It said, *"Don't worry, your time will come."*

Jack merged into the traffic on Main Street, and the car accelerated as Jack shifted from second to third. "Yeah, I guess so," responded Jack. "I think God talks to people."

"Me too," said Phil.

Jack had earned D's in most of his high school freshman and sophomore classes, but as his discipline increased on the track and football field, his confidence grew; and as his confidence grew, his focus improved at school. He was strong and could run fast. Phil was going to college, and others told Jack he could go as well; and maybe, because of his athletic talents, universities would look beyond his early academic years. Everything clicked his senior year when he earned all A's and averaged nine yards per carry on the football field, but Jack tore a hip muscle early in the track season and managed only four races that year. He peaked at the State Championship with a 47.7 quarter mile—the third fastest in history for a high school athlete. Ironically, the two faster times were run in the same race, and Jack placed third.

Phil would attend Brigham Young University in Utah, and Jack visited several universities on the merits of his athletic abilities. He was too much of an academic risk for Stanford. Oregon was impressed with his SAT scores but made no offer, and the University of California at Berkeley was willing to take a chance if he attended summer school, which he did. Jack became a California Golden Bear. Jack's employers, Bill and Bob Griffith were both *Cal* alumni and avid Blue and Gold fans. They were thrilled!

Jack sat in class at Berkeley the first Monday after high school graduation. Tuition was free in public universities, but the compounded expenses of food, housing, books, and clothing added up. Jack felt the pangs inside his chest when he sold the Chevy, but he had to focus on his studies. He performed well.

Jack returned to Woodland for a short break. Bill invited him to visit the store. The brothers asked Jack about school, football, and his plans. When the small talk waned, the brothers looked at each other. Bill pulled a white legal-size envelope from his pocket and handed it to Jack. "This is for you," he said, smiling.

Jack, perplexed, opened the flap, reached in, and pulled out a check. His eyes widened. He looked at the brothers, who smiled back. He read the words on the line. "Six hundred dollars!"

Bob noticed Jack's curious look and explained, "It's a gift as if you had worked every day this summer."

Jack said a silent prayer of gratitude and remembered the day the Griffiths interviewed him as a boy when he had decided to tell the truth.

CHAPTER 4

Jack Who?

It's easy to see where a boy can suffer an athletic injury to his character... From his junior year in high school, he has been subjected to pressures and publicity. He has been led to believe that he can get something for nothing; that life is going to be all primroses merely because he can run or jump or throw or shoot baskets or evade tacklers.[8]

Coach Brutus Hamilton

As a child, Jack lined up with the other boys next to the wooden utility pole that sustained electric cables strung across Fourth Street. He positioned his right foot forward, cocked, ready to sprint, and his left foot waited to explode from behind. Joe Zaragoza took the snap. Jack turned to cut back and meet the quarterback, who reached out and tucked the road-scuffed football into Jack's ready arms. "A reverse!" the boys on the other side yelled. Jack cut in; the cracks in the uneven pavement flew beneath his feet like chalk lines on the gridiron. The boys on Fourth Street imagined their names splashed across the newspapers: "Football Heroes!" The picket fences stood on the sideline cheering, "Go Jack!"

On the heels of 1952's fleeting summer, Jack reported to ground zero, the boys' locker room, the week before Woodland High opened for classes. Forty-five gangly freshmen stripped to their jockey shorts for the turn-your-head-and-cough physical. He stepped onto the metal scale; the doctor adjusted the balance weights and pulled the sliding T-bar down to Jack's head. In those days, the coaches assigned boys to teams based on age and size. Jack was five feet and three-quarters of an inch tall and weighed a hundred twenty-five pounds. The doctor wrote something on a piece of paper, handed it to Jack, and pointed him to the next station, where the coaches assigned him to the Midgets, the smallest of the groups. The trainer took the paper and exchanged it for a set of yellowing shoulder pads. Jack lifted the pads, examined them one way, breathed in the musty smell of fourteen seasons of adolescent sweat, turned them over, and looked at them again. *Which is the front?* Jack had no idea how to put them on. Frustrated, he dropped the equipment on the floor, exited the locker room, and walked home with his chin down as he kicked at the pebbles. *Maybe next year*, he thought.

"Martha" was not her real name, but it was what Jack called her because the sign read "Martha's Bakery" on the storefront. He worked at the bakery the summer of 1953, between his freshman and sophomore years. Martha was a large, rotund German woman with a pink freckled face, her hair pinned in a gray bun. She wore a white baker's dress protected by an apron spotted in a patchwork of stale bread dough and yellowing pastry creams. Work started at five a.m. Jack was surrounded by the heavenly aroma of leavening yeast, bread hot out of the oven, and the sweet blend of fruits, frostings, and butter. He swept the bakery's floors and washed the pots and pans, stopping only for breakfast — Martha had promised him all the donuts, buttery croissants, and warm pie he could eat. Jack began with a small tray of pastries in the corner, eating more each day, and over time, the small tray grew into a full table. Stuffed cream puffs and cold milk were Jack's favorites.

Jack kept his bakery money in a glass canning jar beside his bed. He folded the bills, pushed them in the container, and drew the coins from his pocket, adding them to the collection. Jack smiled as he watched his savings grow. He picked up the paper comic book he kept next to the jar, thumbed through the action-packed pages, and stopped at the Charles Atlas advertisement. Mr. Atlas was the magnificent muscle man, smiling ear-to-ear and standing strong in his leopard shorts. The ad read, "I turned myself from a 97- pound weakling to the world's most perfectly developed man. And I can change your body, too!"

Joe trembled, his ribs protruding, and a sinister bully pounding on the scrawny boy. Joe's girlfriend, Helen, turned away in shame. "Don't let him hit you, Joe!" she pleaded. In the next frame, Joe walked home alone and ordered Mr. Atlas's book.

Weeks later, Joe returned to the beach flexing his new and bulging biceps. "You're a bag of bones!" he shouted to the bully and leveled his rival with one punch to the chin. Helen, from under the beach umbrella, cried out, "What a he-man after all!" Jack would be just like Joe.

Strong Muscular Body
Popular with Girls
New Handsome Looks, Bulging Arms & Legs
Success in Sports & Life

Jack found an advertisement for barbells in a sports magazine, filled out the order form, inserted his savings in an envelope, and walked to the post office. His P.E. teachers and coaches had warned, "Anyone who lifts weights becomes bulky and slow," but Jack ignored the advice. It made sense that he needed to be strong.

Anticipation of the weights stretched the four waiting weeks into a lifetime. It was like Christmas, birthday, and the first day of school all rolled into one when the crated box arrived at 122 Fourth Street. Jack found a hammer, pried open the staples, and organized the weight set in the backyard. He lifted every night. The strain on his muscles, coupled with blood pumping through his veins, invigorated him. He lifted until his calloused hands bled, but his body craved more, so he hammered a two-by-four across the shed door for a pull-up bar.

Combined with Martha's pastries and a growth spurt, the weightlifting helped Jack gain thirty pounds that summer before returning to football. This time, a confident young man walked into the locker room, and again the coaches assigned him to the small team. Jack looked at the shoulder pads, looked at the other boys figuring them out, and he turned his around, lifted them over his head, and dropped them over his neck like an old sweater. *I will play football,* he said to himself, *even if I have to play on the Midgets.*

Jack cherished the afternoons of running, catching, tackling, and blocking. He loved the warm breeze, the smell of turf, and running the ball. While the coach leaned against the chain-link fence and watched the varsity squad through the crisscrossed patterns of the wires, the young boys behind him played as if back on the street. Jack was faster and stronger, and the coach offered to move him to the B team. Jack declined, knowing he would sit on the bench when all he wanted was to play.

Through his junior year, Jack's growing body needed more calories than he could find at home. The pharmacist at Leithold Drugs concocted a thick brown mixture of peanut butter, coconut and soy oils, wheat germ, and whey, the same high-potency potion prescribed to old folks at the rest home, and Jack drank one of these daily. The weightlifting, the pull-ups, the pastries, and whey shakes added hard muscles to Jack's lean frame.

In the spring of Jack's junior year, he ran the quarter mile in fifty seconds flat, faster than any high school student in Northern California. He had grown bigger and stronger and had proved himself ready for the varsity football team in the fall. The Woodland High team had exceptional athletes who, as young boys, had grown up running, jumping, racing, and tackling each other at Beamer Grammar School. As seniors in high school, Manuel Contreras could run the 110-yard hurdles in 14.2 seconds and drop kick a 40-yard field goal. Jack averaged nine yards per carry for a new school record, and several of his teammates went on to play college ball. Armand Jacques, Woodland's student body president, would go to Stanford; Ray Tolson became a guard at Iowa; Gerald Traynham was a tailback at USC, and Jack found himself at the University of California with high school teammate John Bogart.

The *Cal* freshmen played a three-game schedule against UCLA, USC, and Stanford. Jack stood on the sidelines for the UCLA game until the coaches called for him on the last play of the game. After the game, as Jack trudged alone up Bancroft Way, he thought of years of practice, effort, and sacrifices to play football. Emotion swelled within, and he fought the tears of disappointment as he approached his fraternity.

The next game, against USC, Wayne Crow was injured early, and Jack went in as a halfback. He scored three touchdowns, including a thrilling seventy-eight-yard run. Jack's teammates patted him on the back, and his coaches seemed pleased. At the Stanford game, he was anxious to show what he could do against the cross-bay rivals, but Jack stood watching for the first half. He listened to the half-time locker-room adjustments, and he remained standing for the rest of the game.

Jack was confused, his disappointment returned, and he wondered whether he should play football next year or focus on track, but after several players failed their classes and dropped out of school, Jack's place on the team improved. He was on the California varsity team the following year.

Jack took pleasure in college practices as he had years before when he played on the Midgets. He ran the field, made hits, tackled, caught the ball, and felt the sting of sweat in his eyes and its salty taste in his mouth.

He sprinted every drill to win and ran his plays hard. When the coach demanded push-ups, he did more. If teammates dogged in practice, Jack pushed harder. When he ran the ball, he pushed for more yards and hit the defense hard. He became an expert at running the opponents' offenses against California's first team. Maybe the coaches would see how hard he worked.

Jack Yerman, no. 41 University of California

California played Michigan State in its second game of the 1958 season. The pollsters had tabbed the MSU Spartans as the fourth-best team in college football, and Jack planned on sitting comfortably in Berkeley, eating popcorn and listening to the game over the radio. He had no worries — until Wednesday — when the coaches called him over, "Yerman, you are going to Michigan." Jack was the third-fastest quarter-miler in the country, and if they could get the ball to him running around the end, he could turn on his motor for good yardage.[9]

Thursday morning, Jack's roommate shook him awake, "Hey, they called from the airport and are holding the plane for you!" Jack had slept in.

"Uh-oh!" Jack threw on his clothes, grabbed his bag, and rushed to the coaches' frosty glares. He wondered why they had waited.

This would be Jack's introduction to the spectacle of a big game. He marched up the aluminum steps and boarded the piston-powered Douglas DC-6 airliner chartered for the football team. The athletes took their seats, the engines sputtered, and the props began to spin. The plane rumbled down the runway, lifted in the air, and headed for Michigan at twenty-thousand feet. The "stewardesses" chitchatted with the boys; Jack helped himself to several desserts, smiled, and reclined his seat. Jack commented to a teammate sitting next to him, "I could get used to this."

The visiting California team practiced in an old field house made of massive interlocking wooden beams. In front of the facility sat a campus newspaper rack. Jack's eye caught the large block letters of the paper: WORLD TEETER-TOTTER CHAMPION VISITS MSU. Last spring, teammate Jeff Snow had teeter-tottered 148 hours and 43 minutes without stopping.[10] "Yes, indeed, we sure have earned Michigan State's respect," mused Jack.

The quarterback and co-captain, Joe Kapp, was the most celebrated player on the *Cal* team. Joe stood six feet and four inches tall, weighed a solid 235 pounds. Joe's future was bright; he would become the only quarterback in history to be an All-American, lead teams to the Rose Bowl, the Canadian

Football League's Grey Cup, and the Super Bowl. Joe was already a big-ticket draw for this game.

Friday morning, the press waited for the team. Joe walked onto the practice field to a clicking cacophony of cameras. The players nudged closer to Joe and smiled for a photo-op. One in the press shouted, "Hey, Joe, could you throw a pass?"

"Sure. Someone go out." Two fullbacks went in motion for a pass, one from the right and the other from the left. Neither wore a football helmet because, with Joe near, there was a chance of having your picture taken, and Mom, or your girlfriend, would recognize you in the newspaper back home. Smiling for the cameras, they cut sharply across the middle and crash, smashed into each other, their heads colliding like coconuts. Both fell to the dirt floor.

Wayne Crow, the first-string halfback, heard the commotion and rushed from the locker room. He stepped onto the field-house floor and into a drain hole. His body continued forward while his foot remained lodged and twisted in pain. Players and coaches surrounded the mayhem, trying to understand the confusion, and trainers rushed to the wounded like medics on a battle-field. Those with head injuries counted fingers held up in front of their faces, and soon, the three athletes had a bandage or a wrap covering a cut, a bruise, or a sprain. The bewildered coaches gathered for a short meeting, and Jack heard one of them ask, "Jack? Jack who?" Jack smiled and waved.

Buck McPhail, the backfield coach, approached Jack like a salesman, "Son, do I have an opportunity for you!"

"Yes," replied Jack, "I'm in the game tomorrow. But, Coach, I know only MSU's plays." Coach Buck reassured Jack that he would teach him California's offense before the next day.

The team cleaned up and went to a John Wayne movie while Coach Buck, with a pad of paper and a pile of playbooks, met with Jack in his hotel room. The coaches had made adjustments, moving fullbacks to the halfback position, and assigned Jack to play fullback for the game.

As Jack looked over the scouting reports, one player stood out over all others on the Michigan State roster:

No. 88 SAM WILLIAMS ***** 6'5" 235 lbs.

Sam had five stars by his name, was the highest-rated player on the Michigan State team, was the team captain, and played both offense and defense. The Los Angeles Rams had drafted young Sam out of high school, but he had headed instead for Michigan State only to drop out and join the Navy to be named to the All-Military Service Team twice during his four years of active duty before returning to Michigan State – older, meaner, tougher and an All-American.[11]

This game against California would be the beginning of a tremendous football career for Sam. He would be named an All-American in every poll and become a twenty-eight-year-old rookie with the Los Angeles Rams before playing for the Detroit Lions as one of the "Fearsome Foursome."

The Michigan State stadium reverberated the passion of sixty-thousand partisan fans, and "plenty of music from some 35 high schools bands, and a recently returned student body full of Spartan prep and fire."[12] Thousands more sat in front of their radios. Among them listened Jack's grandmother at home in Woodland, who had never attended a game. He could not let Gram, Joe, or the coaches down.

Joe approached Jack: "If we win the coin toss, the first play will be a power right sweep. Do you know what to do?"

Jack had done his homework, "Sure, Joe. I know what to do." California won the toss. The play featured several options: The right halfback would split to the right, leaving the left halfback and Jack in the backfield. Initially, Kapp would take the snap and move along the line to the right. The right end would not block the defensive end but slant for the linebacker. Jack's job, at 180 pounds, was to block Sam Williams. If the big man went for Kapp, Joe would flip the ball to the California halfback coming around. If Sam went for the halfback, Joe would keep the ball and cut up the field for good yardage.

It was the first play of the game, and California had the ball. Thousands of Spartans chanted, "Defense! Defense!" And Jack was on the field. He looked across the line and measured his target. Williams looked even bigger than his description in the program. Jack backed up a couple of extra yards to build momentum. Joe called the count, the ball snapped, and Jack blasted for his collision with Williams.

That was all he remembered.

Later, Jack saw the film. Sam had refused to cooperate with *Cal's* plans. Not knowing what the *Blue and Gold* was up to, he crushed the *Cal* end behind the head with an arm blast, dropping the man to the ground. Big Sam turned to see Jack coming at him, head down at full speed. Sam put his arms together and ripped upwards, catching Jack under the chin and propelling him to a backflip. The California halfback had the ball by this time, and Big Sam, like a professional wrestler, picked him up, showed him to the crowd, and threw him five yards back down the field. Jack felt a plangent pounding in his head and sensed the presence of people around him. "I think he's dead," a voice said. Another joined in, "Look at him bleed!"

All Jack could see was a distant beam of light. "What's wrong? Am I dying? No, maybe I'm going blind!" The ringing in his head subsided, and he realized the circle of light was his helmet's ear hole. Williams had smacked him hard, splintering Jack's facemask, and the helmet had twisted halfway around his head. The septum between Jack's nostrils tore, bleeding all over his new uniform. The referees called a timeout, maybe the longest ever in a college football game because California had no more fullbacks. Jack had to be repaired.

The trainers worked their magic, the bleeding stopped, and they gave Jack a fresh jersey. He walked back onto the field, close to Williams so he could see what had hit him. Sam's massive arms hung by his sides. They were thick, covered, and Jack took a step closer for a better look. Sam had plastic sewer pipe taped around his forearms!

"Hey, is that legal?" Jack asked the ref.

Football players in the 1950s were experimenting with protective gear as padding evolved from thick cloth and leather to plastics. "You wouldn't want him to hurt himself, would you?" said the official as he looked away and blew the whistle for the game to begin. California avoided Sam's direction for the remainder of a long game and lost 36 to 13. The University of Michigan, Pitt, and Illinois studied the *Cal* game, watching Jack fly through the air. Sam's trading card years later recounted, "Most of the time opposing teams would avoid running to Sam's side of the field. Those who did try to probe his area had almost no success."[13]

Jack played sporadically throughout the season, but no one could keep up with him whenever the coaches gave him the ball. The Sunday, October 12 edition of the *Oakland Tribune* dedicated six photographs and a third of a page to Number 41 and the final California touchdown in the victory over Utah:

> Fleet-footed Jack Yerman, the 440 star who plays halfback, crashed over his own right tackle and raced 36 yards to a touchdown in the third quarter yesterday at Berkeley. The Bears finally won the game, 36-21.[14]

Hearts pounded a little faster, people stood a little taller, and they leaned a little closer when Jack ran, broke a tackle, and cut across the field. The campus newspaper added:

> [Yerman] is one of America's great middle-distance runners. His best times are 46.5 in the 440, 21.2 in the 220, and 9.7 in the 100-yard dash....

Yerman's feats on the football field this season have
been something to behold. He has carried the ball
18 times for 124 yards and a 6.8 average, the highest on the team. Jack was a letterman halfback in
1957, and started at right halfback this year, but
injuries to fullbacks Bill Patton and Walt Arnold
forced coach Pete Elliot to move Jack to fullback.
And he has responded very well at that position....

He was selected Player of the Week by the Daily
Californian sports staff after his fine performance
against Utah. [15]

The *Cal Bears* dominated the Pacific Coast Conference, beating
Washington State, USC, Oregon, UCLA, Washington, and Stanford. The cov-
eted Rose Bowl in Pasadena, "the granddaddy of all bowl games," culminated
the season. New Year's Day, 1959, one hundred thousand spectators filled the
Bowl wearing California's blue and gold or Iowa's black and gold. The nationally
televised game was set for 2:00 p.m. The mild Southern California weather
added to the timpani of collegiate drums and fight songs filling the air.

Margo Brown, a vivacious brunette, her younger sister, Karen, and her
Cal sorority sister and hometown friend, Jan Smith, sat among the throngs
of students in the California rooting section. The girls had driven 120 miles
from Taft to Los Angeles in the Browns' little blue Renault Dauphine — a
car distinguished by its two horns: a guttural city horn and a shrill country
horn. They had painted the California mascot, Oski the Bear, on the hood of
the car and joined tens of thousands of fans driving south over the winding
Grapevine that connected the San Joaquin Valley to the Los Angeles basin.
Fellow fans honked in approval at the girls, and the coeds honked their two
horns in return all the way to Pasadena. The stadium's green grass and crisp
white lines glowed from within the sea of blue, black, and gold supporters
for California and Iowa. Margo pointed to a player, "Hey, there he is!" It was
number 41, Jack Yerman.

Judy Crownover, Jan Smith, and Margo Brown—behind the wheel

(Jack and Margo Yerman Collection)

The Hawkeye attack and the Winged-T formation proved too powerful for the smaller Golden Bears. Iowa prevailed 38 to 12. A disappointed Jack had played a token two minutes. Jack knew *his time had come*, and although football had been a childhood dream, it was not to be part of his future. The Rose Bowl* would be Jack's last football game. Bigger and better things awaited on the horizon.

---

* 1959 Rose Bowl Newsreel:
  https://bit.ly/Rose1959

CHAPTER 5

The Girl

You now face three major decisions. First, the university which you wish to attend; second, the profession which you wish to follow; and third and finally, the girl with whom you wish to share your life. I refuse, of course, to have anything to do with this latter decision in any case. However, I might say in passing that there is no dearth of charming, brilliant and high-charactered girls on this campus, should you decide to cast your lot with us, and should you evidence an interest in such distracting items.[16]

Coach Brutus Hamilton

Jack's eyes were burning. His head ached after three hours of studying. Berkeley attracted the brightest students in the nation, and Jack had some catching up to do. He set his books aside, stretched his arms to the ceiling, and walked downstairs. The "exchange," as they called it, between his Chi Psi Fraternity and the Sigma Kappa girls grew louder as he descended the stairs; the music from a Buddy Holly record on the basement Magnavox permeated the house. Jack headed to the fraternity kitchen for something to eat. There, he found his football teammate, Don Piestrip, animatedly chatting with a dark-haired and witty coed. She was drinking milk that Don had given her from the fraternity refrigerator.

She looked at Jack. "Hi, my name's Margo, Margo Brown," she said, tilting her head slightly and smiling.

Margo Brown
(Jack and Margo Yerman Collection)

He shook her hand, "Hello, I'm Jack." He later learned that she came to the party as a favor to her roommate, Diana, a senior sorority sister who had been given the assignment to attend. Margo did not drink, and this event was about beer.

She recognized Jack, "I'm surprised you live here," she said.

"Yeh, me too, sometimes," he replied. The Chi Psi house was where book people lived, not a jock fraternity.

"I saw you at the track meet," she said. "You're the guy who sleeps on the grass."

Margo, a freshman, had followed track since high school and had attended Saturday's meet with her friend, Doug, who worked as a hasher in her sorority's kitchen. They had sat on the backstretch of the track where Doug said true fans sit. "Watch that guy down there," he said. "Can you believe that Yerman? He's only a sophomore, *and man, can he run*! Look, he's sleeping! How can that guy sleep?"

It was a breezy California spring day, and Jack lay stretched out on the grass, seemingly unconscious to the activity around him while other athletes paced back and forth, fretting about the race. Jack had perfected the power-nap before it had a name and slept until the call came from the loudspeakers. He eased up, pulled off his sweats, and jogged to the starting line. "Watch him," Doug said. "Yerman likes to come from behind."

Margo observed the sophomore's cool manner. Just as her friend had said, Jack made his move at the 220, caught the other runners at the 330, and won the 440 race.

Lively music wafted up the hallway and into the kitchen. Jack adjusted his black, horn-rimmed glasses. Margo noticed his movements. "I didn't know you wore glasses," she remarked.

"They're new," said Jack. "I don't always wear them when I run — I just wear them when I need to see!" Jack was running out of things to say, but he wanted the conversation to continue. "Would you like to dance?" he asked.

"Sure!" she smiled.

They navigated between people and made their way to the basement bar. She liked his jitterbug, and he liked her smile, but neither wanted to stay for long. "Hey," said Jack, "would you like to check out my friend Jeff Snow. He's in front of Bowles Hall trying to break the world teeter-totter record!"

"Let's go," she said, and the two escaped into the evening air, talking as they walked.

Some in Margo's hometown described the former beauty queen as "the prettiest thing to have come out of Taft since the discovery of crude oil" and "the reason desert wolves howl at night."* Margo had learned kindness, charity, and prudence from her mother, boldness from her father, and poise from the countless civic functions she attended. She was intelligent, cheerful, beautiful, an honors student, and her calendar booked far in advance. Jack and Margo tried to set a second date over the next several weeks between his travel schedule and her busy calendar. The best they could do was an occasional bag lunch together at the library or at her office, the newly created ASUC Publicity and Public Relations organization, where she would soon become the director.

Jack's times on the track continued to improve. He was third in the NCAA championships, and Coach Hamilton suggested he run the open 440 at the 1959 AAU National Championship Meet in Bakersfield. The meet was only forty miles from Taft, Margo's hometown. Her parents, Bruce and Della, would be there with her to watch him run. "Oh, and be sure to take your passport to the meet," Coach Hamilton advised. "If you run well, you might go to Europe." Coach Hamilton, in his wisdom, had his top athletes carry passports. Having one could be the difference between making the team or not.

Bakersfield can be warm in the spring. Della fanned herself with the program. "There's your boy, Della," Bruce said as the runners congregated on the track.

"Which one?" asked Della.

"He's in lane three," said Bruce, pointing to Jack.

---

* *A high-school friend drew a character of Margo and this is a quote from its caption.*

"Oh, Bruce, he's awfully old, isn't he?" said Della wrinkling her nose. Jack's thinning blond hair was cut short and reflected the silver rays of sunshine from a distance. Jack was nineteen.

The Bakersfield stadium was familiar to the Browns. A year prior, Margo, as Miss Kern County, had awarded the medals to the winners of the National AAU meet. She remembered the first winner, a young black man who leaned over as she placed the medal around his neck; assuming she was supposed to, she planted a congratulatory kiss on his cheek. A meet official grabbed her by the elbow and pulled her aside. "Miss Brown," he whispered, "you can't do that!"

"Do what?" she said.

"Kiss the negro boys," he said with some agitation in his voice. "It's not right — and some people will get very upset." His comments puzzled Margo, who did not carry the prejudices of the earlier generation, but she refrained from kissing any of the winning athletes from that moment.

"First call, men's open 440," the man announced over the PA system. Margo's thoughts returned to Jack, and Della stretched her neck to get a better view of her daughter's friend. The athletes congregated near the starting line. Bruce, Della, and Margo cheered as Jack ran and finished third.

Jack met Margo and her parents after the race and climbed with Margo into the backseat of Bruce's 1956 blue and white two-toned Ford Fairlane. The two-lane highway from Bakersfield to Taft rolled forty-five miles over the desert terrain. Jack would need to be back in Bakersfield by ten the next morning for a meeting. Still, in the meantime, he would enjoy the Brown's hospitality, Della's inquiries, and Margo's undivided attention.

Margo Brown, representing Kern County,
welcomes Vice President Richard Nixon.

(Jack and Margo Yerman Collection)

Because Bruce measured special events by the quantity and quality of food, and he had heard that Jack ate voraciously, he planned to be a gallant host at 410 E Street in Taft. Bruce filled every corner and recess of the refrigerator, which would have burst if it had not been for the latch holding the door shut. Jack awoke to the sound and smell of sizzling bacon and sausages. Stacks of pancakes, a platter of eggs, toast, syrup, and butter covered the Formica table while the refrigerator hummed with relief. After breakfast, Margo drove Jack to the Bakersfield Inn for the meeting. It felt good to sit behind the wheel of "Daddy's" car as they leisurely drove the two-lane highway and talked. They hoped Jack would receive an invitation for a summer travel tour.

Margo was familiar with the layout at the inn, having served as queen of a cosmetology convention some two years earlier. They sat in the hallway and talked while waiting for instructions. A man with the red, white, and blue Amateur Athletic Union logo over the pocket of his blue blazer walked up to Jack and asked, "Is your name Yerman?"

Jack stood up and shook the man's hand. "Yes, it is."

"I understand you have your passport," said the official.

"I do," said Jack.

"Well, you will be leaving for Switzerland in two hours."

By now, Margo was standing as well, and she looked at Jack in disbelief. Margo turned to the man. "How can he? He doesn't have anything here. His bags are in Taft!"

"You'd better get his things, ma'am," he prodded, and, turning to Jack, he continued, "We need to have a meeting in five minutes."

"I can be back in two hours…maybe!" exclaimed Margo as she pulled the keys from her purse and headed for the lobby door. She jumped behind the steering wheel and took off.

Margo crossed a series of four-way stops on her way out of town. The car rocked each time she hit the brakes at an intersection. Each stop seemed to speak to her, "*You're not going to make it!*" Margo's frustration mounted as she reached beyond the steering wheel for the Fairlane's chrome gear shift. Her thought momentarily jumped to the car lot in Los Angeles, where she had watched her dad haggle with the salesman about standard and automatic transmissions. "A man can shift a lot of gears for forty-five dollars!" Bruce said. She pulled the gearshift into first, her foot already on the gas, and the car leaped forward across the intersection.

She heard the unmistakable whine of a siren and saw the black and white patrol car in her review mirror. "Oh, no!" The flashing red light signaled her to pull over.

Margo's nerves were on edge. Her plans for the weekend had changed suddenly, her folks would be disappointed, and Jack was leaving in less than two hours. She broke down in tears in front of the officer.

"Young lady, you know you're not supposed to be drag racing," he explained in a deep voice.

"Dragging? Who's dragging?" demanded Margo between sobs. "You and that other car that's pulled over there!" said the officer, pointing to a vehicle that had also been detained.

Margo had been unaware of anyone else on the road. "I didn't even see that car," she explained.

"Miss," he said, "you pealed out pretty fast."

"My boyfriend's leaving for Europe in less than two hours, and he can't go unless I get his suitcase." Margo gave the officer the quick story.

Maybe because she was a former Miss Kern County, or because her father was a volunteer sheriff, or because of her tears, the officer paused, looked at Margo wiping the moisture from her face, and said, "OK, I'm not going to give you a ticket. You can go. Drive carefully — but you'd better hurry!"

She hit the accelerator, and a tail of dust lifted from the road's shoulder. Jack had phoned ahead, and Bruce was waiting at the curb with the suitcase in hand. He passed it to Margo, who climbed into the backseat while Bruce took the wheel, and Margo's younger sister, Karen, rode shotgun to watch for California Highway Patrolmen. Margo rummaged through Jack's clothing, selecting and refolding what he would take to Europe for the summer.

Forty-five miles later, they pulled alongside the idling Greyhound bus with Jack waiting outside. "Oh, thank you!" a relieved Jack said as he pulled the suitcase from the car.

"Do you have any money?" asked Bruce.

Jack looked in his wallet. "Three dollars," he said.

Bruce pulled out a twenty-dollar bill, all he had, and handed it to Jack. "Don't spend it all in one place!" he said with a smile.

Jack accepted the money, shook Bruce's hand, gave Margo a quick hug, and boarded the bus for LAX.

Jack had learned that he was part of a six-man American team competing in Europe. The world-class athletes included Ray Norton, the 100-meter world-record holder; Bill Nieder, the soon-to-be world-record holder and Olympic champion in the shot-put; Elias Gilbert, the world-record holder in the 220 low hurdles; Bill Westine, a seven-foot high jumper; Tom Courtney, the Olympic 800-meter gold-medal winner, and world-record holder; and Jack, the 440 runner who happened to have his passport. The six eager athletes flew to New York and then to their home base in Lausanne, Switzerland.[17] The Americans would visit nearly every country in Europe and run a meet every two days before joining a full United States team for the first-ever track meet with Russia — behind the Iron Curtain in Moscow.

The rush of leaving California and Margo's family had left Jack contemplative. He had not expressed, in person, some things that he hoped to share with her. He liked Margo, and before leaving New York, Jack sent a heartfelt letter:

June 24, 1958

My Dearest Margo,

In the rush of leaving, I did not have a chance to say many of the things I wished to tell you. It is perhaps best that they were left unsaid until I see you again. I would only like to say now that knowing you has altered my life considerably. I find myself treating people with greater consideration and understanding....

After my hasty departure from Bakersfield, the team went by bus to Los Angeles, where we flew all night to New York and today have been seeing the sights and getting visas.

I think I know how badly you felt when I had to rush so last Sunday. You had looked forward and planned for the weekend, and you were hoping that we might be able to enjoy ourselves together. My brief encounter with your family was short, and I hope that no poor impressions were created.

I must apologize for this letter. I am very tired and haven't slept since I saw you last. I understand why the Americans seem to fall short of top marks on these tours. The guys are a real swell bunch.

Love you always,

Jack

The Americans rarely lost an event in Europe, but they could not stack up enough points to win a meet without the depth of a team. For example, the June 28 Lausanne meet program listed the 6 Americans and 113 Swiss athletes competing.[18] This was good for the European press. Newspapers reported victories as local athletes, who finished second and third, compounded more points than the Americans, who, when sober, usually finished first. Jack did not drink and ran well most of the time. Back home, the newspapers praised the small U.S. team:

> **ZURICH, Switzerland,** July 2 (AP). U.S. track and field stars whipped the rain and the Swiss yesterday, winning four of seven events in an international meet.
>
> With most of the track under water and the 4,500 spectators drenched by the constant downpour, Jack Yerman of Woodland, Calif., won the 400-meter race in 47.5. Tom Courtney of Livingston, N.J., the 800 meters in 1:52.4. Elias Gilbert of Winston Salem, N.C., the 200-meter hurdles in 25.4 and

Bill Nieder of Lawrence, Kan., the shot put with a throw of 16.67 meters, 54 feet 2 inches.

Swiss athletes won the 200 meters, 110-meter hurdles and the high jump.

Ray Norton of Oakland, Calif., pulled a thigh muscle and did not compete in the scheduled 100 meters.[19]

At a meet in Lausanne, Jack promised to run the 800 with Tom to pace him to a new world record. Jack would take the lead. Tom would follow step-in-step in Jack's draft. At the appropriate moment, Tom would take over and sprint to the finish. Jack shot out of the starting block like a rabbit. He ran the first 400 with Courtney tucked behind Jack's shoulder. Jack could hear Tom's rhythmic breathing. He knew Tom was strong. At the 600-meter mark, Jack pulled to the side. To the delight of the crowd, Tom sprinted to the world-best time of the year.

The American athletes became accustomed to the routine of unhurried parades, girls marching with colorful flags, and long speeches before the meet. The six young men chitchatted with the crowd, posed for photographs, and smiled all-American smiles for the enthusiastic Europeans. Fans collected autographs as Americans collect baseball cards. Young boys and old men surrounded Jack with treasured autograph books.[20] Jack wrote to Margo and reported running in the rain and on muddy tracks. He described Switzerland as a "green and fresh garden." As any young man might, he took note of the lake near their quarters and was impressed with the bathing attire. In a letter to Margo, he teased, "The water is too cold to do any serious swimming. I might say, however, that I am more convinced that you should get a bikini. The girls wear them, and the suits—they don't look half bad."

When the team boarded the train and crisscrossed the Alps to a meet in the northern Italian city of Milan, Jack was sick. He had been stung by an unknown insect while jogging in the woods. The bite had festered in his thigh to an infected battle of fever and puss. Jack could not bow out of his obligation to run, nor was quitting in his nature. He was scheduled to race against Panciera, the pride of the Iberian Peninsula. While the other Americans were untouchable, the Italian had a fair chance of beating Jack.

The team arrived at the train station expecting an escort to the hotel but found none. Their ever-present Swiss host hailed two taxis and herded the group to a five-star hotel. After they had unpacked their bags, the athletes went off to see the city, leaving Jack in bed to calm his fever. Jack's head felt soggy as he drifted in and out of sleep. The ache in his leg migrated to a pounding in his temples, which he eventually realized was a knock at the door. He got out of bed, limped to the door, and opened it to find a man speaking broken English. The man introduced Jack to a woman dressed in a white nurse's uniform. The meet directors had learned that an American runner was ill and had sent help. Jack welcomed them. The woman placed medicated hot compresses on his contaminated leg and gave him a shot of antibiotics. The attention alone seemed to make Jack feel better. He had hopes of beating the determined infection.

The boys returned from sightseeing to find Jack's spirits higher and shared with him marvelous sights of Milan: the world's largest cathedral, the masterpieces they had only seen before in books, and the delicious foods. While the athletes talked, they observed a persistent hotel porter who would enter the open door for a moment, look around, leave, and return to repeat the same routine. Bill Nieder, the street-smart, muscle-laden six-foot-eight shot-putter, was determined to discover what the impish fellow was doing. "On that guy's next visit, he's going to tell us what he's looking for," exclaimed Nieder.

When the mole returned, Bill cornered the man, who looked up at the towering athlete and noticed several battle scars across the American's face.

"What do you want in here?" demanded Bill.

The tiny man protested that he was innocent of anything but doing his job. To Bill, who thought little of diplomacy, the answer was not convincing.

Bill grabbed the little Italian, carried him to the third-floor balcony, flipped him over, and hung him by his feet over the traffic below. The blood flowed downward, and the porter's face reddened.

"I talk! I talk!" cried the tiny man. Bill pretended to drop him an inch.

"I tell you what you ask!" screamed the man with greater urgency; Bill pulled him back into the room.

The Americans learned that big money had been wagered on the 400. The local Mafia knew Jack was sick, and the odds had gone from three-to-one for the *Americano* to five-to-one for the *Italiano*. Gamblers tried to find any edge on the odds, and the porter had been hired to keep close tabs on any changes in Jack's condition. Bill sarcastically smoothed the wrinkles out of the little man's jacket and sent the porter away. The stunned team looked at Bill, who turned to Jack and asked, "How are you feeling?"

"Better," said Jack

"Can you beat this guy?" Bill questioned.

The fever had broken, his leg was moving better, and the swelling had decreased. Jack, who was fundamentally strong, and with a couple of days until race night, replied, "I can beat him."

With a growing smile, Bill turned and said to the team, "We're going to get that money!" He called each of the boys by name and said, "Give me your money. I'm going to get it back for you and more." He took the cash that each had saved from his three-dollar daily allowance. "Don't let anyone enter this room until after the race," Bill demanded, "and Jack, if you leave the room, you limp on that bad leg. When you warm up at the track, you limp again!" Bill pushed their money into his pocket and left the room.

The Italian officials hoped for the publicity of a big meet. A man approached the Americans during practice with a curious proposition: if Tom pushed their ace 800 runner to an Italian record, the Americans would earn a trip to Rome. Courtney mulled over the offer. After thinking for a few moments, he agreed to the proposal on one condition. "I want to see the Pope," he said. The man agreed, but on the night of the meet, Tom learned there would be no Papal encounter, nor would there be a friendly reception from the Italian spectators. The gun sounded the start of the 800, and Courtney walked around the track waving to the crowd, who hissed and booed at the American. The temperament in the stands deteriorated further. Everyone, it seemed, was in a disagreeable mood for the 400-meter race. The restless mob surveyed Jack and argued over who would win. Some in the impassioned crowd placed bets. Jack could see the tattered Italian Liras passing from one person to another.

Yerman on right, Panciera on far left

(Jack and Margo Yerman Collection)

Jack sucked in a deep breath of evening air and smelled the freshly cut grass. His leg felt better, and he knew he had a good run in him. Jack pretended to limp, just as he had promised, and shuffled unevenly around the infield during the warmup as he surveyed the ruddy cinder oval. This would be a strange race. Rather than the usual 400 meters around two turns, this track encircled a large soccer field that swelled the track's oval to nearly 500 meters. The stadium lights focused on the center field, leaving the rounded curves buried in shadows. The runners would leave the light and enter the dark bend, only to emerge out the other side, having been concealed for a few seconds from the crowd. The race would finish with a 120-meter sprint in front of the heated fans.

Eight runners were summoned to the far side of the oval track opposite the finish line. Jack knew precisely the lane the powerful gamblers would assign the young American: number eight. Jack looked over his left shoulder to find Panciera in the choice lane – number four. The high-spirited Italian waved to the hopefuls, who would return home that night, brilliantly drunk, bragging of how they had made their money. In their eyes, Panciera raced for country and honor. The spectators leaned over the edge of the track to get a better view.

Like a calculating hawk preying on a rabbit, the Italian had the advantage of observing the American from the inside lane behind. Jack would not see the hunter until the final 120 meters. Tonight, Jack had a simple strategy. He would capitalize on the only advantage the track would give him, the unusual gentle curve of the swollen far right lane. Jack would hit the dark turn at a world-record pace and leave the unsuspecting Italian too far behind to make a move.

The athletes lined up at the starting blocks, set their feet with one slightly forward, knelt in position, and waited for the gun to crack. It fired, and Jack pushed forward as he had hundreds of times — but this time was different. The starting block blew apart into a confusion of pieces, and Jack stumbled to find his stride. Someone had tampered with the equipment. Jack could hear the runners and the spitting cinders from teethy spikes ripping into the track. He knew he was behind. Trying to recover, he pushed fast on the cinders, and they pushed back. Jack approached the dark curve, felt a surge of power as he hit the turn's obscure peak, but disaster struck again. Jack felt a sharp pain shoot up his leg as if a bullet had been fired from the ground, cutting through his calf into his pulsating thigh. His leg gave out — body flinging forward — as the horizon moved perpendicular. Jack instinctively ducked his head, rolled over his shoulders in a flying somersault, and returned to position without losing a step! It was a move he had learned years before from Robert Allen, a grammar school football coach, and Jack was upright just in time to see Panciera pass him as they reemerged into the light. The Italian had a ten-meter lead with 120 meters to go.

Jack's adrenaline surged. Every sense heightened, his vision clearer, his running sleeker, and he exploded after the Italian. He sprinted off the curve to the final straightaway at the feet of the maniac crowd that pelted him with food and rubbish reeking of alcohol. Jack focused on Panciera with the vindictive instinct to win. The hunted was now the hunter. Three meters, then two, one — the crowd screamed. He heard Bill yell something. Jack leaned forward at the tape and won by inches. Jack was clocked at a world-class time of 46.8 on an unusual track. Panciera was right behind at 47.7. The disappointed fans quieted. [21]

What happened on that turn? Jack brushed the dusty cinder off his jersey and walked back to the dark curve. His eyes adjusted to the shadows as he bent down to feel the track. There they were — a cluster of malicious round holes strategically dug four inches deep in his lane. The holes were invisible in the dark cinder. He could have broken his ankle or blown out his knee and ruined his career.

The following day the team boarded the train for Switzerland. Bill was talkative and cheerful, but neither Jack nor any of the other athletes ever saw their money.

Jack returned to Berkeley in the fall, and his relationship with the darling, dark-haired coed grew closer. Margo, like his high-school friend, Phil, was Mormon. Margo invited him to join her for a regional conference. They walked the steep Berkeley hills to the church on Sunday, where Jack discovered several congregations meeting together. He listened as everyday people gave inspirational messages. Jack was at ease with the "Latter-day Saints" who lived Christian lives, followed a code of health, smiled easily, and seemed grounded to good things. His Methodist foundations were not so different than what he had experienced in Margo's church. Jack asked Margo to line up some lessons so he could learn more. Jack met with two local graduate students who served as missionaries in their spare time.

Jack's fraternity house was neither convenient nor private, so they met in a "date room" at Margo's sorority. Margo, knowing this would be Jack's journey, excused herself. After the third lesson, the missionaries asked if he would pray and ask for himself what direction he should take. Jack read aloud the New Testament verse in James:

> If any of you lack wisdom, let him ask of God, that giveth to all men liberally, and upbraideth not; and it shall be given him. (James 1:5, KJV)

Jack remembered his discussions with Phil, and believing that God answers prayers, Jack scooted off his chair and knelt with the graduate students in the middle of the dating room. He watched the girls, bowed his head as they did, and reached into his soul for the courage to speak. He said, "My Heavenly Father…" A peculiar, warm sensation filled his soul. "I even teared up a bit," he later shared.

At that vulnerable moment, the door swung open. A sorority sister stopped abruptly, and Jack bolted to his feet. She pulled herself back, "Oh, I'm sorry!"

The moment was over. Jack's complicated schedules of school, work, football, track, the Olympic Games, ROTC Officer Training, and Boot Camp pulled him in several directions. He would not see missionaries again for two years.

CHAPTER 6

To Russia with Love

I hate to see sports used in a kind of political propaganda, and I hope that our own country can remain civilized enough never to stoop to this.[22]

Coach Brutus Hamilton

The world was frightening and unpredictable in 1958. The United States and Russia were at the height of the Cold War, and the United States set the rules for a dangerous game: *We have the bomb, and you don't. If you don't do what we say, we get angry and drop our bomb on you.* The Soviet Union soon joined the game and tested a big bomb of its own. Now, the game was more complex: who could make the biggest *"boom?"* The United States exploded a nuclear weapon, and Russia responded with one bigger and better. The bombs grew fatter. The US blew holes in the bottom of the Pacific Ocean, and at one point, disintegrated an entire island. The Soviets responded by firing a bomb into the stratosphere so powerful it would have blown a hole a mile deep and five miles round if on Earth. Russian military shot at American pilots taking secret photos over Soviet air space. In two more years, the Soviets would bring down U-2 pilot Francis Gary Powers, who would sit in prison until an exchange was arranged for the Soviet master spy Colonel Rudolf Abel, who had set up a spy network in New York City. Brinkmanship, the policy of pushing a dangerous situation to the brink of disaster, had set humanity on a catastrophic collision course.

President Eisenhower and Premier Khrushchev signed a *détente*, a French word meaning, *Let's relax a little and pretend to be friends*. Governments in both countries had fed people misinformation, and as a result, the Americans and Soviets were ignorant and afraid of each other. Some hoped that cultural exchanges might help the superpowers become a little friendlier. With *détente*, Stalin's Iron Curtain would open for the first time. Dark-suited diplomats in far-off places discussed exchange options: the Russians wanted the American track team, and the Americans asked for the renowned Bolshoi Ballet. These were the circumstances that led to Jack's participation as one of the youngest members of the first American team to penetrate the Iron Curtain.

As a member of the small American team traveling through Europe, Jack, at age nineteen, had lived a celebrity summer competing in remarkable cities, tasting new dishes, and signing autographs. During that same period, the U.S. national team had spent much of the torrid summer waiting at West Point, confined to a routine of tedious training and wondering whether the Soviet meet would happen. "How would the Soviets use the event to their advantage?" "Would the Americans be safe?" At the last moment, the dark-suited men decided that it would look bad for Moscow if the track team could not compete.[23]

Officially, the U.S. team was seventy-three strong, including the coaches, and was the largest delegation of American track-and-field stars ever assembled outside the Olympics. The team included six previous Olympic gold medalists.[24] The Soviet press reported that the meet was sold out — 104,000 spectators would fill the stadium, and the Russians would not discredit themselves by demonstrating against the United States at the meet.

Jack's small touring team met the U.S. national team in Helsinki. Instead of the seventy-five athletes and coaches he had expected at the airport, there was a sea of two hundred people waiting to board the three planes. "Why such a large group?" Jack asked an athlete. He was told that many were government officials — State Department and trade officials, likely including CIA, some piggybacking on the team to enter Russia.

The team waited all day at the airport. When Jack asked why so long, the answer came back, "The Russians want us to arrive after dark." The sun descended to the horizon with hints of orange and purple peeking through the evening clouds. A small fleet of planes sat at military attention with wings staggered in formation and bellies open, awaiting the American athletes. These were not the modern jets that Jack had expected, but Russian *Lisunovs* — small, twin-engine tail-dragging imitations of the American fat-bellied DC-3 workhorse. The Russians would not allow American aircraft over the Soviet landscape, just as anxious Americans feared Aeroflot overhead.

These young athletes were America's pride and possibly the most talented track team ever assembled — an army of crusaders sent to proselytize democracy in well-pressed charcoal-grey travel slacks and smart-looking skirts, white-collared button-down shirts for men, and matching blouses for the women. Jack's narrow red, white, and blue tie fluttered in the gentle breeze as he stood waiting with his blue USA sports bag at his side. The officials announced that it was time to board the planes; former Olympic athletes, world record holders, and officials to the front, and others, like Jack, found themselves in the last group. He walked to his assigned plane, stepped from the tarmac, and ascended the metal staircase. The barren interior reminded Jack of an old Bluebird school bus with stiff, upright seats. He chose a seat near the entrance, thinking a quick exit might be beneficial if the engines failed.

The planes lined up and took off one by one. "Last on" means "first off," so Jack's plane led the squadron of metallic birds over the Russian landscape. As the ground drifted away, Jack felt uneasy, thinking of the young American soldiers who only days before had stormed Lebanon's beaches to restore stability to that troubled country. "American Colonialism" brought heated responses from the communists who had organized angry demonstrations for the world to see. Jack wondered how the team would be received in Moscow.

From his bird's-eye view, Jack watched grass-roofed barns flowing under him. He saw an occasional farmer working his way home before nightfall, and he could almost see the definition of each shingle on the country homes. Jack soon understood the reason they had been crowded into the old planes. The Russians, who controlled the route and altitude, had been careful to prevent the Americans from taking photos of anything significant. Dusk faded into night, and the Soviet pilots maneuvered the planes towards rows of kerosene torches held by soldiers signaling the outer limits of freshly graveled runways built for refueling on this trip. Young soldiers hurried from the shadows, rolling fifty-five-gallon drums and hand-pumped fuel into the thirsty planes.

The fleet approached Moscow, a city of six million people. Jack's plane hit the tarmac and taxied to the hangar, and the pilot opened the door. Jack unfolded himself from the plane, stood in the doorway, and breathed the summer night's air. He looked for the other aircraft with the Olympians and diplomats, but they were nowhere to be seen. It occurred to him that he would be the first American the Soviets would meet, and he felt it his duty to represent his country and team. He descended the steps, lifted his right arm, and waved to the gazing Russians with his all-American James Dean smile. Two beautiful girls approached, reminding Jack of USC cheerleaders, except for their white blouses, knee-length plaid skirts, and lacy cottage aprons. The girls placed an abundant bouquet of fragrant flowers in Jack's hands. The blond girl leaned over and kissed him on the cheek. He felt his face flush and his heart thump.

The blond girl spoke English with a crisp British accent, introduced herself, and explained she was studying tourism at the University of Moscow and worked for *Intourist*, the official state travel agency. Jack later learned that *Intourist* was founded in 1929 by Joseph Stalin and staffed by KGB officials and would grow to be the largest travel agency in the world.[25] The agency managed foreigners' access to and travel within the Soviet Union. The blond girl stopped for a moment, looked around to affirm that others would not hear her, lowered her voice, and whispered to her new American friend, "Do you believe in God?"

Jack looked at her curiously, "Yes, I believe in God," he said, realizing at that moment her question sprang from the state of affairs in the USSR. Lenin had once said that "religion is opium for people," a "spiritual booze,"[26] and to believe in God, in Russia, was for the old and unsophisticated.

The blond girl looked around again and then turned to Jack, "Do you live in a cottage?" In her world — the Moscow that Stalin had built — a private home, even a tiny cottage, would be a luxury. The city's masses lived behind a monotonous blend of repressive cement apartments where mothers, fathers, children, neighbors, newlyweds, the old, the sick, the strange, and the innocent shared kitchens and bathrooms for the benefit of the State. As Jack would soon learn, duplicitous doormen, often women, held all the keys to the apartments and kept watch, signing tenants in and out. They noted in their books the arriving rations of meat, vegetables, flour, and cooking oil, even a small piece of cake delivered to a cherished grandmother. Nothing was private.

Jack thought about his childhood and home on the other side of the world. Mom, Gram, Kathy, and Jack had all shared the same bedroom. Jack had slept in the baby crib until he was six and then, for a time, shared the bed with his sister at night — the same bed where Mom slept during the day. As the children grew, Jack needed his own space away from the women. He converted the eight-by-ten-foot slat-board shed in the backyard to a bedroom.

Fixing the Roof on Jack's Backyard Shed

(Jack and Margo Yerman Collection)

He had pushed his bed to the low end of the sloped ceiling, crammed rags in the knotholes to slow the penetrating cold from the damp winter, covered the walls with newspaper, repaired the roof, and slept under layers of blankets. It was *his* cottage, a space where he could dream, think, read, and grow more confident until he left for the university. Jack was unexpectedly overwhelmed that his humble home would be a luxury in Moscow. "Yes, I live in a cottage," he said.

The aircraft carrying the Olympians and the diplomats arrived. The group boarded the waiting buses and headed towards Moscow's evening lights. Russia had not opened its doors in decades. The American athletes were the first significant group to be welcomed at the capacious Leningradskaya Hotel, an enormous facility reaching the sky with hundreds of empty rooms. The bronze lattice entrance, the carved-timber ceilings, the chandeliers, and the lion sculptures could not hide the hasty construction. The travel-weary Americans expected prompt service and room assignments, but the unpracticed Russians were not prepared for a crowd. In the confusion, Jack was the only athlete assigned to a room on a floor separate from the rest of the team. All others were assigned to the floor above.

Jack went to his room, laid his tired body on the hard mattress, and thought of home. Woodland was like other small towns in the United States where children watched newsreels and TV warnings of radiation maps and potential mass destruction. Children practiced duck-and-cover drills at school. Evacuation signs marked the quickest routes out of the big cities. City councils designated cement basements in town halls and libraries as safe zones, and Middle Americans built fallout shelters of their own. Jack shut his eyes and resolved he would be an exemplary American. As Jack drifted to sleep, he considered that he might personally prevent World War III by making a Russian friend.

The athletes had five full days before the meet. Much of that time was spent dozing in the hotel or training while the Russians filmed the American workouts.[27] The Americans began to explore Moscow. On the way to Lenin's tomb, Jack made sure to smile warmly and talk to everyone, but it was challenging to have a conversation even though crowds followed the team trying to speak English. "Hellow, jou look like a Russian," some would say, but a conversation was not what they wanted. They simply hoped for a reply.

The Americans began to drift all over Moscow, and Jack still needed to make a friend. He decided the best option to unite the Russian and American worlds was to befriend the *dezhurnaya*, his maid, with the keys, who sat at a desk in front of the elevator on his lonely floor. She was the epitome of an ageless, wrinkled Russian grandmother, standing a little more than four feet tall with beady gray eyes and a little bun on top of her head. Each time Jack walked to his room, she handed him his key attached to a heavy steel ring attached to a solid metal ball.

Even though he smiled his biggest smile and said "*Da*" to the Russian key keeper, she did not respond. *Maybe she's afraid of me*, he pondered. People in the Soviet Union lived in fear of the KGB, with its secret operatives, masters of disinformation, torture, and assassination. Jack ran into Russian fears when he and decathlete Rafer Johnson attempted to shoot home movies with an 8mm camera. When the Americans walked to the market, Rafer lifted his camera only to be met by a fist-shaking crowd that turned on the Americans and shouted angry words in Russian. Later, Jack tagged along with hurdlers Ancel Robinson and Hayes Jones to a neighborhood of dilapidated row houses that dated back to the turn of the century. The residents surrounded the athletes, and one angry man, in broken English, demanded, "No photos!" The Russians seemed ashamed of their paucity and did not trust the American visitors. The athletes retreated, and Jack had yet to make a friend.

The team visited GUM on Red Square, the oldest department store in the world. To an American who could shop at Woolworth's or Sears, this place was barren. GUM reflected the dearth of the Russian Five-Year Plans, which explained why Jack had been approached several times by people offering fifty dollars for his used Levi's. Amid this meagerness, Jack realized he could bring some joy to his maid's lean and colorless life by showing the souvenirs he had collected from all over Europe. No doubt she would be fascinated with his little trinkets, perfume, silks, toys, and glass. Jack decided he would place a map on her desk, point to the places he had visited, and if he gave her a gift, he would make a friend.

Jack collected the trinkets from his room and set them one by one on her desk next to the map. The Russian grandmother responded with "*Da*, *da,*" but was not enthusiastic. "Maybe she's a little frightened," thought Jack. "This isn't going to be easy."

Jack had another idea. While visiting the U.S. Embassy commissary, he had bought root beer, peanut butter, and cashews. Jack left the map on her desk and ran back to his room. "She is going to have the treat of her life!" He grabbed the can of cashews and sprinted back to Grandma Russia's desk, with the nuts clanging up and down in the can. When Grandma saw the streak of red, white, and blue racing towards her, her beady black eyes widened. She reached for the collection of keys and took off in the opposite direction. Jack shifted gears to race pace and chased after her. Her low center of gravity gave her the advantage — she was moving fast, her keys jangling, and Jack pursuing her with cashews rattling in the can. She hit the doorway and disappeared. By this time, Jack stopped his pursuit and laughed, "This is my first race behind the Iron Curtain, and I lost!" He returned to his room, opened the can of nuts, breathed in the scent of sweet cashews, and ate a few in her honor. He pulled off his sweats, collapsed in his bed, and slept.

Somewhere, when sleep was at its deepest, when the body was at its most gratifying rest, long before the sun rose — *Bam* — Jack was thrust awake by silhouetted invaders brazenly crashing through a now wide-open door. Blinding lights seared his blinking eyes as he pulled into focus the pointed barrels of a pair of Russian automatic rifles. The squarely dressed, uniformed major barked, "Jou are vunder arrest for attempting to assault jour maid!"

Assault? Am I going to be shot? Jack was bewildered. The soldiers pushed their guns into the American. He saw the pear-shaped woman glaring from behind her brigade—clutching the keys in her fat little hands.

The major peered at Jack, back at her, and then back to the American. The soldier's lips curved to a smile for a moment and then back to his serious form. The major belted, "Impossible! But jou vill come with us." Jack pulled on his sweats, and the soldiers marched him to the end of the hall and through the exit. Their army boots pounded up the steel staircase to the U.S. team's floor, advanced down the corridor, and stopped in front of a door. The old woman followed along, shifted her keys, and found one to fit the lock. She turned the pins and opened the door. The soldiers threw Jack's belongings inside and motioned for him to enter, "Jou vill stay here." It was dark. Jack smelled the semisweet acrid sweat of a well-seasoned athlete. He hesitated for a moment, flipped the switch, and the light fell down the walls, across the twin beds, and over his scattered belongings. This room belonged to Harold Connelly, the 250-pound, handsome, gregarious world-record hammer thrower.

Harold was not a man who understood the word "no." His tenacity began at birth. He set the record for the heaviest baby born at Somerville Hospital in Massachusetts at twelve and a half pounds, but his size made delivery difficult. He dislocated his left shoulder and crushed his brachial plexus nerves at birth. Harold fractured his feeble left arm thirteen times as a child, and consequently, it grew to be four and a half inches shorter than his right, and his left hand two-thirds the size. Harold would say, "They didn't treat the disabled with dignity then. I couldn't stand to be treated differently.... The thought of being patronized made me sick. I wanted to play by the rules, not rules adapted for me because I was disabled." [28] Like Jack, Harold had discovered weightlifting in his early teens and that it would help him overcome his weakness. Harold had soon excelled at the shot put and football in high school. He attended Boston College and volunteered to help the hammer throwers retrieve hammers. "Before long, Harold was throwing the hammers back to the teams' throwers farther than their throws into the field." [29]

The hammer is a symbol of strength, coordination, and agility. The athlete propels a sixteen-pound metal ball attached to a handle by a four-foot-long chain. The thrower spins three or four times in a ring and flings it. What Connolly lacked in arm strength, he made up for with speed and leg power, and when he won the gold medal in Melbourne, 1956, photographers yelled to him to raise his arms in victory. Harold lifted only his right arm. [30]

Harold met beautiful Olga Fikotová, the Czechoslovakian Olympic discus champion and the pride of the Soviet Block, in Melbourne. The talented youths talked and spent time together at the Olympic Village. Harold spoke to Olga in fragmented German, and she responded to him in broken English. Their curiosity developed into a friendship, and their friendship into romance.[31]

Connolly proposed marriage a few months later. The Cold War relationship between two gold medalists could not have been more complicated and required diplomatic intervention. The U.S. Secretary of State, John Dulles, announced at a press conference, "We believe in love," but the Czechoslovakians were less willing. Olga would later share, "It was unheard of at the time, and the [Czech] government didn't know what to do with it. They rather unpleasantly told me what they thought about being a traitor."[32] Harold suggested that they both write a letter to President Antonín Zápotocký. The president granted Olga an audience and warmly received the Olympic champion. As they talked, he cautioned Olga that if she were to go to the West, she would forget her country and "sell out to the American glitter."[33] Olga loved her homeland and explained she would honor country and continue to represent Czechoslovakia in sport. She simply was in love with another athlete who happened to be an American and requested permission to marry.

President Zápotocký listened and said, "I cannot help very much because different offices make the decisions. What do you want me to do?"

"Just do whatever you can," responded Olga. "If you can put in a kind word, I'd be most grateful."

"I'll tell you what," said the president, "you have my blessing, and I'll put in a word for you."[34] A few days later, Olga received a permit to marry a foreigner.

Harold visited Prague in 1957 following a European goodwill tour for the U.S. State Department. The two planned a quiet wedding in the middle of a week, hoping to stay under the authorities' radar and protect her parents from the negative attention. Despite their efforts to keep the ceremony a secret, word got out, and thirty thousand people turned up in the town's square to celebrate. "People sang and cheered and walked along with our wedding party," recalled Olga. "When the Prague police officers smiled and waved and asked people to let us walk through, I realized this was an extraordinary moment." [35]

The Czech government issued permission for Olga to emigrate to the United States. Harold sold one of his hammers to buy tickets, and Olga traveled with a government-issued paper of official signatures and bureaucratic stamps. She realized something was wrong on the express train to Vienna when, at the border, everyone had a passport. Olga knew little about travel documents and never had a passport. The controlling Communists had always carried their athletes' documentation to prevent defections to the West.

When the newlyweds arrived in the United States, they reported to the Czech embassy in Washington to meet the ambassador and regularize Olga's paperwork. Olga intended to keep her promise to the president and represent her country at the European Championships. She assumed that she would exchange her official paperwork for a proper passport and a visa. When she explained her predicament and handed the paper to the ambassador, he looked at it, paused, sat back in his chair, and glared at the young athlete. "We do not expect you to traipse around the world," he said.[36]

Olga sat stunned as she realized that without a passport, she would not travel and could not keep her promise to the president.

It was Harold's turn. He took advantage of the trip to Moscow, the control center of the Soviet Union, to obtain a visa for Olga, and now Jack was in Harold's room. Jack did not know that wires were embedded in the plaster carrying noise through the hotel's walls and back to Soviet ears. Unseen listeners heard Jack wonder out loud, "Where's Harold?"

The sun's warm rays announced morning through the window. Jack rolled over, opened his heavy eyes, and looked across to Harold's untidy bed. The big man was still missing. He sat up, rubbed his face, and cleared his senses in time to welcome a heavy, square woman, barging through the door, yelling and pointing at Jack's mess on the floor. The woman abruptly turned and exited, leaving Jack scratching his head. A few minutes later, the same woman returned, followed by Dan Ferris, the U.S. Amateur Athletic Union chairman with an interpreter. Dan looked over the scene while Jack explained that he had just been trying to make a friend before the commotion started.

Dan listened, looked at the clothes on the floor. "Jack, it's absurd, but just go along with them," he said, shaking his head. Jack picked up and folded his clothes, found places in the drawers and closet, and even made Harold's bed.

After breakfast, Jack headed for his workout at Lenin Stadium. He walked by the corner where the bulky weight men hung out. A friendly arm grabbed him. It was Harold. "Comrade Yerman, you're my new roommate!"

"Yeah, Harold, it's been crazy. Where have you been?"

Harold explained to Jack that because the KGB had bugged the room, and unexpected visitors, like the cleaning lady, were common, the hotel cell wasn't a place he wished to spend his time. When Harold and Jack returned to their room, Harold pointed to the wires peeking through the plaster and to a decorative flower hiding a tiny microphone. Harold placed a water glass over the flower and banged on it with a spoon.

Jack laughed and imagined the reverberations thumping on hidden ears. He leaned over the flower, "Hey Harold," he said, "help me with this new secret code machine!"

"OK, Yerman," replied Harold, "but wait, I can't put this fuse together. Could you hand me that wire?"

Harold was on a personal mission to aggravate the Russians. The same pointy-nosed KGB agent tailed the pair each time Jack and Harold left the hotel. Jack and Harold named their new friend "The Weasel." The agent followed the Americans everywhere. One day, Harold dragged Jack to the Kremlin. Harold opened doors, entered offices, and collected a crowd of anxious bureaucrats who followed the Americans through the corridors until they grew tired and ushered the athletes out. The Russians were direct and clear. No visa would be forthcoming.

Telegram from Margo

(Jack and Margo Yerman Collection)

One hundred thousand spectators filled the stadium on the first day of the two-day competition. The highlight of the meet, the most published event of the competition, was the duel between UCLA's student body president, Rafer Johnson, and Russia's decathlon star, Vasily Kuznetsov. Rafer was the most celebrated athlete on the American team. When he was 16 in California, his coach took him to watch a meet featuring Olympic champion Bob Mathias compete in the decathlon's running, throwing, and jumping; he thought to himself, "What's the big deal with this? And he told his coach,

"I could have beaten most of those guys." [37] His Coach entered him in a high school invitational, and Johnson had been winning ever since. After two days and ten grueling events, Rafer emerged the victor, shattering his own world record and beating Kuznetsov's unofficial record.[38] The Soviets in Lenin Stadium stood and cheered the two decathletes who embraced. The ice of the Cold War briefly softened.

The closing event featured the 1,600-meter relay. Jack ran the first leg in 46.7—fourteen meters in front of his competitor, followed by Tom Courtney, Eddie Southern, and Glenn Davis. The Americans defeated the Russians by forty-five meters on a muddy track with a time of 3.07.0. The American men won the meet with a score of 126 to 109.[39] The American women took four of ten events against the chemically enhanced Russians, but the U.S. ladies lost 44 to 63.

The final score appeared on the electronic scoreboard: USSR 172, USA 170. The Americans were dumbfounded! The Russians had agreed to mark the competition as two dual meets, one between the men's teams and the other between the women, but when the Russians combined the scores, they changed the rules, and the U.S. lost.[40] Communism declared a great victory over democracy; the following day, papers worldwide touted the Soviet win. Jack, like most of the other U.S. athletes, felt cheated.

Jack and Harold headed back to their room, banged their fists on the flower a few times, and made grumpy remarks about Russians into the microphone. The athletes felt better knowing that a spy on the other end was recording their frustration.

Someone knocked at the door. "Jack, are you expecting anyone?" asked Harold.

"No, you?" responded Jack.

Harold moved to the door, turned the knob, and pulled it open. The Weasel, escorted by another Russian, whom the American team knew as

John Roman, stood smiling with a bottle of vodka in hand. John Roman was the lead agent assigned to watch the Americans. Harold looked at the men, then down at the jug. "Come on in," he said.

Drinking is a sporting event in Russia, and two large Russian weight men carrying more vodka strolled into the room behind John and The Weasel. They started drinking and talking to Harold. As the liquor flowed, tongues loosened, and John Roman shared that he had learned his perfect English when he was eleven years old from downed WWII American pilots that he hid from the Germans, fed, and eventually helped escape.

Jack watched Harold raise his jug and match the big men drink for drink. The group talked about World War II, the Iron Curtain, Khrushchev, Eisenhower, the Cold War, and sports. The conversation turned to Olga and what she might do if she ever made it to Czechoslovakia. "She's just visiting family," explained Harold.

At five a.m., the Russians laid unconscious on the floor, and Harold was still going strong. The Americans grabbed their bags and said goodbye to John Roman and The Weasel. They left the hotel for the airport bus and on to Poland. The team left the city limits as the sun burst onto a new day.

The lingering anger from the meet's results had not yet faded. The group exchanged few words as it watched the landscape shift past the windows when, without warning, the bus pulled to the side of the road and stopped. A green sedan rested at a diagonal in front of the bus with its hood towards the road's shoulder. Jack watched the bus driver's white knuckles release their grip from the steering wheel and pull the door lever to allow The Weasel to climb aboard. The agent's bloodshot eyes systematically scoured the group until he found Harold sitting in the back. Without saying a word, he walked to the back and handed Harold a parcel. The Weasel turned and exited the bus. Harold opened the envelope, pulled out papers, and looked through them. He grinned and stood up, "Olga's going to Czechoslovakia!" The bus broke into cheers.

Indeed, Olga and Harold had received visas. Still, they were "transit visas," allowing them to stay in Czechoslovakia to visit her parents only a few hours in the airport until the next plane departed.˙ It would be fifty years before Olga returned home for an actual visit. Harold and Olga worked every conceivable angle to recognize her native citizenship, but they could not break the Cold War prejudices. Olga received a letter from the Czech Olympic Committee stating that it no longer considered her a citizen because she could not train in Prague. Olga recalled, "Then, I realized that I'd been told 'no.' I was crushed, mainly because I'd promised something to the president and had no way to explain it." [41]

Olga became an American citizen, and eventually her parents joined her in America. Olga competed for the U.S. Olympic teams in the Rome, Tokyo, Mexico City, and Munich Olympic Games. In Rome, her former teammates shunned her. She would not understand "why" until eight years later, in Mexico City:

> I learned [in Rome] that somehow everybody was angry with me because the Czech athletes turned away and wouldn't talk to me.... Then, much later, in Mexico City, I met a group of Czech athletes. I looked at them, they looked at me, and so I said hello to them in Czech. They all knew me or had heard about me, and they started talking to me, and then one said, "All right, how was it? Did you really fly the coop, or did they give us a pack of lies about you?" I told them that I hadn't run away and told them what had happened. It was only then that people began to understand that it had only been claimed that I had refused to compete when, in fact, I was not allowed to compete. [42]

---

*   *Jack spoke with Olga in 2012 to verify this information.*

Olga's proudest moment as an athlete came at the 1972 Olympic Games in Munich when she carried the American flag at the opening ceremony. She said, "I believe in a democracy that the flag belongs to everybody, so I felt like I was representing every person in the United States." [43]

Fifty years after earning her country an Olympic gold medal and a world record in the discus, the Czech Olympic Committee reunited her with teammates in her homeland. Olga said of the occasion, "My emotions are high. I'm overwhelmed to tears. I think it's extremely gracious, and I'm happy." She added, "I believe in the Olympic Games. I believe in the Olympic ideal. I believe that the Olympics will survive spiritually. I think I've given a lot of my life to promoting the Olympic philosophy of brotherhood and sisterhood of humanity." [44]

CHAPTER 7

The Rendezvous

[A young man] must have good stuff inside to keep his wits about him. He is called upon at eighteen to make decisions which would challenge those much older and wiser. It is to the everlasting credit of our athletic youth that so many of them turn out well in spite of so many temptations put in their way.[45]

Coach Brutus Hamilton

The flight to Warsaw, Poland, was short. The team arrived at its hotel before noon. Four hundred friendly Polish fans asking for autographs surrounded the Americans. Twenty-two thousand would watch the dual meet over two days, and Jack would run against the fastest 400 sprinter in Europe that night. He was tired from last night's negotiations and needed rest. He pushed through the mob, received his room assignment, and slept.

Wham, wham, wham...

Jack was startled awake by a rapid knocking on his door. *What now...?* he wondered. Jack staggered to his feet and cracked open the door to find Dee Givens, the Oklahoma State sprinter, greeting him with an ear-to-ear smile. Dee, who had been injured in practice and would not run, had decided to occupy his time sightseeing.

"Yerm, you're my bud, aren't you?" demanded Dee in his distinctive southern drawl.

"Yeah," Jack said, wiping the sleep from his eyes.

"Then get your stuff on. I need your help. I've got us a *rendezvous* with two girls, and they won't budge unless I get a friend, and *you* are my friend."

"I'm tired, Dee, and I have to run tonight," Jack replied. "Well, just come and take a look. That's all I ask," said Dee.

Jack groaned, invited Dee to wait for him, and put on his street clothes. Dee led Jack out of the hotel to a small corner cafe. Two petite, cute, full-bodied girls with bouncy poodle haircuts sat waiting in a booth. One was a redhead with green eyes and the other a blue-eyed blonde. Jack wasn't tired anymore.

"Jack, I'll take the redhead; you can have the blond," announced Dee.

The attractive girls offered to show the boys the city. They helped the Americans exchange money on the black market. Jack's pockets bulged like a hamster's cheeks that had just found the mother lode. He hired a taxi for a dollar a day and bought a steak lunch for twenty-five cents. The girls took the Americans to the remnants of a Jewish World War II ghetto and to a workshop that made expensive Polish glass.

Jack and Dee decided to show the rest of the team what a couple of real operators could accomplish in a short period. They gave the girls tickets to the track meet and made plans to take them to the black-tie dinner honoring the Polish and American teams after the meet. The Americans performed well. Jack won the open 400 and ran a fast 46.2 in the second leg of the 4x400.

After the meet, a taxi dropped off the two couples at the hotel. The "men" strutted down the hallway to the grand ballroom with their dates clinging to their arms. The doorman welcomed Jack and Dee, announced their arrival, and placed their invitations on the silver tray. All eyes focused on the girls, but Jack was not prepared for the glares that followed. Conversations halted; it was as if the tinkling of champagne glasses stopped, and the orchestra faded. An angry Polish official rushed over and ordered, "Get those girls out of here. Now!" The girls cried, strong Polish words were exchanged, and the boys pulled the girls back to the street and hailed a taxi.

Jack could not make sense of what had happened, nor did he understand what the girls and the official had said to each other. The sobbing girls would not disclose anything. Jack felt at odds; instead of showing up at the party like a couple of operators, he and Dee had embarrassed their dates. They decided to rescue the evening and take the girls to a nightclub. The nightclub was in the basement of a stone-grey gothic castle dating back to the fifteenth century. The girls excused themselves to the powder room, leaving Dee and Jack to discuss the evening. A stranger approached the table and introduced himself as a British national working for Reuters News Agency. With a touch of antipathy, he queried, "What do you know about those girls?"

"Well, they *are* pretty," Dee responded with his broad southern smile — his eyebrows lifting.

"Yes, they are stunning, but do you know *anything* about them?" asked the man.

"No, we don't really know anything," interceded Jack before Dee could boast again.

The man pulled out his business card and wrote a phone number on the back. He gave it to Jack with instructions, "I want you to call this number at the American Embassy and ask for Major Brock. He's the Marine Security Officer and will have some information for you." The man turned and was gone.

The boys walked over to the black phone box hanging on the wall. Jack inserted a coin, turned the dial marking the numbers, and the phone rang: "American Embassy, Sergeant Smythe speaking." After talking to a second sergeant, he waited until Major Brock came to the line. "Who are you, and what is the problem?" His demanding voice sounded far away.

"We're with the American track team and on a date with two attractive Polish girls," explained Jack.

"Describe the girls," barked the major over the scratchy connection.

Jack described the blond and the redhead in detail.

"Do not wait to hang up," insisted the major. "Move! Get out of there! Do not talk to those girls. You are the targets of two female Polish secret-police agents. *They want something!*"

"Thank you, sir," responded Jack in his best ROTC voice. Jack hung up, turned to Dee, and looked directly at his eyes. "We run!" he said.

"No," Dee argued. "No way. We stay. I'm from Oklahoma, and I know how to handle this."

Jack never understood what sort of special knowledge boys from Oklahoma had in dealing with Polish secret agents.

"Jack, listen to me," Dee retorted, unfolding his arms to free his hands for exclamation. "You see, we know who the girls are, and the girls don't know that *we* know who *they* are! Let's tease them for a while. It'll be fun."

The girls walked back to the table. Their makeup was back together, and their confidence restored. Jack and Dee quickly learned what their dates wanted. They would be vindicated if the boys would take them to the next party at the American Embassy. Jack surmised that the girls had hoped to become familiar faces at the ball and would be invited to other U.S. parties later. They wanted access to people, specifically embassy diplomats.

At Dee's persistence, the boys decided to see the girls again the next day. The girls continued to apply pressure for an invitation to the party. Later, Jack told his date what Major Brock had reported and believed she was with the Polish secret police. She protested, "No, I am not!"

The boys said their goodbyes and would not see the girls again.

Two years later, Jack sat reading a magazine at Bancroft Library on the Berkeley campus. A recent spy case had made national news. It confirmed Major Brock's warning to the boys. On December 5, 1959, it was Irvin Scarbeck's turn to work the night desk at the American Embassy in Warsaw. He was alone, the phone rang, and he picked it up. A young woman's voice greeted him — a rich, whispery Polish accent speaking English. He had been warned to beware of phone calls from strange women. "It is a favorite approach used by lady spies," they had told him in his orientation. The young woman on the phone asked something about a visa, and he decided it would be best to deliver the information personally. He planned to meet her on a nearby street corner.

He found the girl — her blond hair cut in the popular bobbed style of the day. Her large eyes were soft and inviting. She laughed easily, and she stood close to the middle-aged diplomat. Her rose perfume captivated his senses and heightened his awareness of her tight sweater and short skirt that left little to Irvin's imagination. His devotion to his German wife and their three children faded in her mesmerizing presence. He asked her name.

"I'm Urszula Discher," she said. She was twenty years old and explained that she lived in the back of a store, not far from where they stood.

He planned to rendezvous again. He eventually rented a private apartment for her on Koszykowa Street in Central Warsaw, two blocks from the American Embassy, and they began a fourteen-month romance.[46]

On the evening of December 22, 1960, Communist agents broke into the apartment and photographed Scarbeck and the girl together in bed. The Polish police threatened to jail her on charges of being an unregistered prostitute. Irvin Scarbeck was the second secretary at the embassy. He was responsible for much of the daily operations as well as having access to classified information. Two Polish officers known to him as "Zbigniew" and "George" threatened to jail Miss Discher and expose the American if he did not provide classified information to save his unfortunate lover. He succumbed to their demands.

Irvin explained to Urszula that the work of spies was a chess game, and he would find a way to get her out of Poland. He arranged for a friend in West Germany to send a telegram to Urszula claiming her non-existent brother lay dying in a Frankfurt hospital. Scarbeck negotiated with the Polish authorities and traded more secrets to obtain a visa for the girl. Urszula flew ahead of her man but went straight to a Frankfurt boarding house used by Communist agents as a secret rendezvous.[47]

Scarbeck was reassigned to Italy and was unaware that American counterspies had placed microphones in his office and had collected the needed information to arrest him. He was summoned to Washington for meetings. FBI agents descended upon him as he walked the capitol's streets. Urszula was extradited to the United States to testify at the trial. Scarbeck claimed that he had betrayed his country only to help the young woman escape Poland. He refused to believe that she was involved with the secret police. The whole of the United States was riveted on the titillating scandal, and every small-town newspaper printed a photograph of the fair Urszula Discher and carried news of Irvin Scarbeck's conviction and thirty-year sentence to prison — the first American Foreign Service officer ever caught in a treasonable act. Shortly after the trial, the young girl, who previously had wanted out of Poland, quietly returned to Warsaw.

Decades later, Rink Babka spoke to Jack at the 2011 Mount Sac Relays banquet in Pomona. The U.S. 1960 Olympic track team was honored for breaking five world records and six American records at the tune-up meet before leaving for Rome. As the men sat reminiscing, Rink asked Jack, "How did two guys like you find such cute girls in Warsaw on that trip?" Babka had been the team ladies' man, handsome, and the best dressed, and he still wondered, half a century later, how Jack and Dee had found the blond and the redhead. Jack shared the story with Rink and mused, "I wonder, what ever happened to the redhead?"

CHAPTER 8

Would the World be Different?

You can blame the [Berkeley] student strike for this long screed. I am presently in the Dean's office, but the building is closed, and all appointments have been canceled while the staff tries to clean up the mess following yesterday's sad and bewildering events. The building is a mess.[48]

Coach Brutus Hamilton

In the spring of 1959, Jack's junior year at Berkeley, he had extra time on his hands. Jack had decided not to play football to prepare for the Olympic Trials, and without the routine of practices, scrimmages, or team meetings, he needed something to do — something that would make money. When Jack learned that the student body president earned a respectable $3,000 a year, he decided to run for political office. Where the student council met was a mystery to him, but he needed a job, and he believed that no one truly cared who the president was. "Hey, I can win this one," he told Margo. Although she had doubts, she signed on as his campaign manager.

Margo worked with the Associated Students as Director of Student Publicity and Public Relations. She knew something about student government, so, with her help, Jack set off to conquer the ASUC presidency. They began by meeting with an ex-president, Roger Samuelson, and developed a platform that proposed more married-student housing and invited renowned speakers to the University.

The candidates grew to three: Dan Lubbock, a member of several clubs, John Schaefer, a pre-law and business student, and Jack, with "No affiliations with any radical, fraternal, or conservative political group," wrote a reporter in the campus newspaper.[49] Jack and Margo followed the traditional Berkeley campaign pattern: "Take the candidate to the students." Margo took Jack to the sound of clinking silverware and glasses, the aroma of baked potatoes and gravy, and an occasional, "Please pass the salt." Jack and Margo visited students in dorms, fraternity houses, and sororities who paid little attention while eating dinner. It mattered little because there was nothing remarkable in this race — until Dave Armor showed up.

Dave represented everything that Jack and the other candidates did not. He was a political science major and part of SLATE,* a new campus political party that entered the contest with a candidate for every post and a liberal affirmative action and equal rights platform.[50] The source of SLATE's funding was a mystery, but it had a printing press, rented office space, and mobilized professors and students. The SLATE machine joined the race with deep pockets and challenged the traditional candidates who had few resources and a university-imposed thirty-dollar spending limit.[51]

Armor pressed the ASUC to take a stand on off-campus issues.[52] Jack retorted, "All aspects of student welfare — our interests in city, state, and national issues — should not be pursued by the Student Association." Armor asserted that the sports program should be recreational and managed by the student government. Jack countered, "It would be foolish to put a multi-million-dollar athletic program that brings prestige to the University and its

---

*   *SLATE refers to the "slate of candidates." SLATE is capitalized in documents remembering the movement, although the papers at the time wrote it as "Slate." Both versions are found in this chapter depending on the source.*

students into the hands of novices. Organized intercollegiate sports build character, provide support and entertainment for students, and generate revenue for academic programs. Intercollegiate sports are the showpiece for wider fundraising and scholastic efforts. The program must have a dedicated, dependable, and professional administration."

SLATE candidates spoke out against the establishment and traditions. The University was synonymous with insensitive government; SLATE's defiant rhetoric against the *status quo* moved Student Association President Bill Strickland to request that the University withdraw official recognition from SLATE:

> The University of California must be a place where laws are changed by lawful means, not defied by mob action. It is the responsibility of this university to guarantee that the students who pass through its halls do not leave with a warped view of how lawful society operates. Lawful society demands remedies for the open defiance of laws and regulations.
>
> I request that University of California official recognition be withdrawn from the group of students known as Slate. I further request that University of California official censure be imposed on these individual students who carried out the defiance rally of Thursday, March 12, 1959.[53]

E.E. Stone, Dean of Students, ruled that student groups could not take positions regarding off-campus issues. San Francisco Assemblyman John A. O'Connell requested an informal opinion regarding Stone's ruling from the State of California Attorney General's office. The attorney general ruled that SLATE could not be prohibited from engaging in off-campus political activities, although the University may prohibit the use of its facilities.

Furthermore, the American Civil Liberties Union became interested in the controversy.[54] Powerful groups now had a stake in SLATE's success.

An obscure conflict in Southeast Asia, in tiny Vietnam, had found its way into the newspapers. SLATE argued against sending America's youth across the sea to fight someone else's battles. The Bay Area press began covering the Berkeley campus elections. Meanwhile, SLATE continued to grow, using the off-campus office to coordinate commuter students. The candidates debated in the school's traditional free speech area on the question, "Should *Cal* student government be involved in off-campus politics?"

The excitement grew daily, and a new issue surfaced that brought national attention to the race. SLATE challenged Berkeley students to denounce, and even withdraw from, the National Student Association, which was "a front for the Central Intelligence Agency." "Mr. Armor has gone too far on this one," said Jack to Margo. "We'll get him!" Jack defended the National Student Association as an upstanding organization representing students' interests in Washington. Armor raised the rhetoric, "The National Student Association is a tool of the CIA!"

Jack believed he had the election — until disaster hit. At a press conference on the East Coast a few days before the election, a reporter asked Allen Dulles, Director of the CIA, a question: "There's an election going on in Berkeley where one of the candidates says the National Student Association is linked to CIA. Is that so?" Dulles answered the reporter by acknowledging that the CIA gave the Association money each year for students to study in Iron Curtain countries. In exchange, the CIA received reports on the economy, morale, and structures within those countries. This statement hit Jack — and the rest of Berkeley — like a boulder. All eyes were on the election, and it grew to be the biggest election in the school's history. Jack realized he was out of his comfort zone. He began to fear the responsibility of the office if he actually won.

Tuesday, May 12, a record 5,622 students went to the polls. Armor received 1,769 votes, and Lubbock pulled a close 1,517 to qualify for the runoff. The other two candidates received too few to continue: John Schaefer earned 1,150 votes, and 587 students voted for Jack.[55] The next day, Coach Hamilton, with a grin and a twinkle in his eye, said, "Jack, not many men can claim 587 friends."

Voters found Dave Armor more compelling and voting for SLATE more exciting. Armor won the final election by a slim thirty-three votes,[56] and SLATE took over student politics at Berkeley. Students were ready for a liberal take over; after all, the youth of America supplied the army with its warriors. Many were not willing to put their lives on the line for a war they did not understand.

Looking back, Jack had seen signs that the campus was changing. Berkeley sat on federal land, and as such, required that young men enroll in ROTC. Having grown up in a neighborhood that honored returning World War II heroes, Jack had never doubted his responsibility to participate in ROTC. The government also gave him a uniform that included sturdy black shoes that he needed for school and an extra dollar a day for serving as an upperclassman cadet officer in command of a thousand men.

Each month, on a Thursday, thousands of students, dressed in their uniforms, paraded in front of the reviewing stands. Jack's shoulders were square, and his breast swelled with pride as his men marched in step across the baseball field and made the big turn in perfect order towards the observation deck lined with colonels and generals. On a brisk spring Thursday, Jack's battalion marched as they had done many times before, with heads turned sharply to salute the Sixth Army. To the shock of those in the reviewing stand and to Jack, the men dropped an assortment of women's panties and bras in front of the reviewing area, strewn the length and breadth of the company. SLATE challenged compulsory ROTC enrollment within a year of the election;[57] their timing was perfect.

SLATE toured campuses across the state to propagate its politics to students at UCLA, Riverside, and Santa Barbara. It organized defiant political groups in the face of conservative opposition:

The meeting reached a climax when the UCLA student body president accused Slate of "fomenting strikes and riots."

Slate arrived at Riverside Saturday to find that a warning of their visit had preceded them. Stamped across the top of the student activities bulletin distributed to all students were the words "Beware of Slate"....

[Santa Barbara] Student body president Kitty Joyce said at an executive committee meeting last week "the Associated Students did not invite them and did not want them." A faculty member defined Slate for the council and said it was "a political-action group of students with outside support, which appears to have as its intent the obstruction of virtually every official position taken by the University administration."

He went on to say, "Slate is interested in destroying the University as we know it. We are old enough to get our own show," he said.[58]

Back in Berkeley, unusual people drifted into the city, camping along the sidewalks of Telegraph Avenue. They would later be known as flower children. The youth of America questioned blind patriotism. They challenged the United States' role in world affairs, while others declared, "We won't take anything from those long-haired freaks." The world's eyes remained focused on what Berkeley would do next — and it soon had its first Free Speech riot; then came the drugs, the anti-establishment movement, the civil rights and anti-war movements, protests and demonstrations, and the youth of America crying, "Make love, not war!" Berkeley was at the heart of "groovy." There were "love-ins," "sit-ins," "happenings," and "hippies."

Jack watched the social unrest move across the United States and wondered whether there might be a shrouded scheme to start trouble in America's universities. Indeed, if the CIA could send students to foreign schools through the National Student Association and gather information, why wouldn't other governments do the same — maybe even upset the American establishment?

Several years later, Governor Ronald Reagan used his handling of the unrest in Berkeley to prove his law-and-order stance and gain national prestige. In April of 1969, an eclectic group of young people "reclaimed" a parking lot owned by the University of California.[59] The group tore up the asphalt, planted a garden and several trees, set up a swing set, and built benches. People's Park was born. Reagan ordered them off the land, and when they refused, he sent in the National Guard.

A protestor was shot, and the incident exploded into an insurrection of six thousand people.[60] The National Guard evacuated, and the park remains today as an icon to the counterculture where the flower children, although much grayer and slower today, linger in the psychedelic sunshine of their victory. The University of California's halls whisper echoes of those early activists.

In retrospect, it all began with SLATE — and Jack, having been at the crossroads of the Free Speech Movement, muses, "If I had won, would the world be different today?"

CHAPTER 9

Olympic Trials and Tribulations

It's easy to be intense in competition. It's difficult in practice these cold, rainy and lonesome days. But project yourself forward — these are the days that count. These are the days when champions are made.[61]

Coach Brutus Hamilton

Jack trained through the fall and was feeling good about his running when tragedy struck. His campus job required moving equipment at gymnastics meets. After a meet with UCLA, Dave Epstein, a 440 runner, and Jack pushed the bulky vault across the gym floor. They lifted the apparatus onto a piano dolly and aimed it for the doorway. The dolly jammed on the doorframe, and Dave pushed with a grunt and a shove. The vault skidded off the dolly and landed with a thud squarely on Jack's big toe. "Ouch!" The pain shot up his leg, and he reacted instinctively, lifting the vault off his damaged foot in one swooping reflex. Jack's grimaced; he pivoted on his good foot, his bad foot hovering over the floor.[62]

Jack turned and limped down the hallway to the office of Jack Williamson, the athletic trainer, who gently removed Jack's black and white Chuck Taylor and pulled off his sock. The blood had collected under the opaque toenail, and, as his foot felt the cool air, the throbbing pain crawled up his leg.

"We've got to relieve some pressure," said Williamson. He proceeded to drill a tiny hole through the injured nail, and a mixture of red fluid oozed relief from Jack's swollen big toe. Jack sat on the table, gingerly slid his shoe on, and limped ten blocks uphill to his fraternity. The tender toe continued to swell, and he asked a friend to drive him to the Student Health Services at nearby Cowell Hospital, where he remained overnight. He lost his toenail, a serious problem for a runner. The *San Francisco Chronicle* published a photo with Jack gazing at his foot. The caption read, "GET WELL, BIG TOE."[63]

His condition grew worse when his well-tuned muscles favored the injury, throwing off his muscular symmetry, creating new aches and pains throughout his body. Jack's world-class training program slowed to a remorseful stop. Jack watched his teammates for the next two weeks prepare for the regular season while he stretched and slowly jogged until the swelling and tenderness disappeared and his big toe had healed.[64] Jack began the track season racing against Keith Thomasson, a Stanford athlete who had run a 46.2. Jack had not practiced since the accident. He ran and lost.

Jack trained with renewed vigor. The smell of the track, the crisp spring air, and the spectators wearing hats and sunglasses with programs in hand were all a welcome return to normalcy. He felt strong, just in time for the Pacific Coast Conference meets. Jack's pent-up energies peaked at the Modesto Relays. "I'm ready," Jack whispered as he knelt in the blocks. The cracking sound of the starter's gun produced a visceral reaction, like one of Pavlov's animals, and Jack shot out of the blocks leading all runners to hand the baton to his teammate. His team of four broke the world record in the sprint medley relay.

The Olympic Trials would be held across the Bay at Stanford University. An athlete who finished in the top three of his event would then qualify for the Olympic team. Jack had three opportunities to qualify for the Trials: (1) he could place in the top six at the NCAA championship meet; (2) he could place in the top five at the national open trials; or (3) he could qualify by placing in the top three at the military trials.

Jack decided to run the 400 meters at the NCAA meet held in Berkeley, where he had home advantage, and a week later, he would travel to the AAU National Championships in Corpus Christi to compete in the 800. If he qualified for both, he would decide which to run at the Olympic Trials at Stanford because running both in the 1960 Olympics was not an option.

Head Coach Brutus Hamilton

The NCAA heats at Berkeley were scheduled for Friday, and the finals were on Saturday. Jack felt strong and in shape despite starting late in the season. His times were among the fastest in the nation. Coach Hamilton sat in the stands two days before the meet for a meeting with every college coach that had a runner in the NCAA finals. Jack approached Brutus and asked, "What's the workout for today, Coach?"

"Warm up. Then we'll try a few hundreds."

Jack reported to the end of the track and jogged toward the starting line with his hand raised in the air to signal Coach Hamilton that he was ready;

he accelerated to the line and dropped his hand. Watching from the stands, Brutus clicked his stopwatch and marked it again when Jack sprinted across the finish line in front of the coaches, "9.7." Jack felt terrific and jogged back for another run. He approached the start again, dropped his hand as the aggregate of coaches clicked their watches. He crossed the finish line and heard the collective buzz, "9.6!" A hundred stopwatches clicked in unison when he ran the next time, and a combined "Ooh!" rose from the bleachers. Jack ran a 9.8. Three impressive times back-to-back, and he felt great! Jack continued to run hundred-yard intervals, and the watches kept clicking — Jack's adrenaline, endorphins, muscles, and mind melded together, and consumed in the aura of a runner's high, he whispered to himself, "I can do this forever!"

Jack crossed the finish line the sixteenth time in 9.8 seconds. "Jack, that's enough. It's time to go in," said Coach Hamilton.

"Go?" Jack questioned. "I'm not tired, Coach."

"We'll call it a day, Jack," said Hamilton. "You're ready for Friday."

During the night, Jack's muscles protested and tightened. The fibers in his legs were not ready for the physical intensity his mental resolve had demanded. Morning greeted him with his legs as stiff as fence posts. He sat up and willed his feet to the floor. His calves, his quadriceps, his hamstrings, and his glutes screamed back at him. He could hardly stand. Jack panicked, "How stupid! What am I going to do?" He asked a roommate for a ride to the locker rooms. There, Jack Williamson massaged his muscles, sat Jack in the whirlpool, packed his legs with analgesics, and stretched Jack's muscles. But nothing would reverse the damage. Jack's confidence crashed — again. Neither Jack nor Coach Hamilton realized that getting caught up in running in front of the country's coaches would have such serious consequences; they had showcased Jack's ability, but in so doing, had exceeded his physical capacity.

Only the top four of each of Friday's two 400-meter heats would advance to the finals. Jack felt heavy and managed a third-place with a 47.3 to advance,[65] similar to his high school 440-yard time.

Despite his performance, sports-writers predicted Jack would win the finals:

```
This race is wide open. We pick Yerman because
he's always there when the real running starts,
even though he has no blistering finish...few go
by him in late season. Almost any of the finalist
could win it.[66]
```

Jack's leg muscles screamed in protest and he skipped the warmup. Seven athletes reported to the blocks and six would advance to the Olympic Trials in two weeks' time. He knew that it would take a miracle to beat just one runner — one of the best in the country. Jack knelt in the starting blocks and wished he could disappear. He had no strength remaining in his stiff legs. When the starter's gun fired, Jack staggered to the vertical position in what would be a lightning-fast race. The other athletes moved away from Jack. He had worked for a chance at the Olympics, the pinnacle of an athlete's career. His dream faded with each second, but he pushed as he did years ago when, as a boy, he ran across a freshly plowed field simply to see whether he could do it. He raced against his throbbing muscles.

Jack was five-meters behind the others at the 200-meter mark, fading, and out of contention — but at that moment, a runner grabbed his leg falling to the track. *What's happening?* thought Jack. The athlete's face grimaced. *Had he pulled a muscle?* Jack ran past the injured athlete and miraculously placed sixth to qualify for the Olympic Trials, more than a full second behind Ted Woods of Colorado who set a new meet record, that day.[67]

Few people had known the extent of Jack's injury.[68] Reporters, coaches, and athletes only guessed at how he might run in the trials. Jack remained secluded in Berkeley for the next two weeks, staying at Hamilton's house rather than crossing the Bay Bridge to Palo Alto and training with the other athletes. Brutus cared for the entire wellbeing of his boys; he watched out for them on and off the track. He was like a father — a disciplinarian and a counselor. Coach Hamilton was careful with his athletes, but Jack's debilitating stiffness surprised them both. Brutus's program had already worked miracles in Jack's short season. There was no better place for Jack to become whole again than under the care of Brutus and his wife, Rowena. Brutus had a way of working his athletes to peak at the right time. Jack was fundamentally strong, in shape, and needed to synchronize his mind and his muscles. A week before the meet, Coach Hamilton believed Jack was ready to run harder. They quietly set the schedule to peak the day of the Olympic Trials.

The Trials at Stanford drew the largest crowd ever to see a track meet in the United States since the 1932 Olympic Games in Los Angeles. Sixty-five thousand filled the stadium for the finals with a two-day total of 106,000 fans.[69] Jack won his heat in 46 flat. The final race would be run in less than an hour. The fanatical track nuts argued over who would win. Would it be Otis Davis or Teddy Woods? [70] No one considered Jack a contender, but his training had prepared him for the day's tight schedule.

Other athletes stretched, jogged, paced back and forth, and tried to stay warm between the races. Jack found a shady spot under a training table. He closed his eyes and felt the refreshing breeze drift over his forehead. He rested until the call came for the eight fastest quarter-milers in the country to report to the track.

Each of the eight runners had an individual story of long training hours, obstacles, and a dream of running in the Olympics. Each stood waiting in apparent coolness, but inside, nerves twitched, and minds focused. "Runners, to your marks," called the starter in the white cap. The athletes moved up to the starting blocks. Some shook their arms, others looked to the heavens, and all set their feet in the blocks. The eight runners knelt in position as if praying to a higher source. Jack looked up and focused on the white lines framing his lane. The man lifted the starter's gun. "Set!" he bellowed, and the runners lifted their backs to the sky. The man paused for a moment and then squeezed the trigger.

The eight runners blasted out of the blocks. Arms pumped, and legs flew around the first curve. As quickly as the sweat beaded on the athletes, it evaporated in the speed as they sprinted around the track. Jack was in fifth place at the 200-meter mark. The Bay Area track fans had seen Jack come from behind in other races. Knowing spectators pointed and predicted, "Now watch this Yerman. You will think he's part of the pack, and then toward the end, he'll pour it on."

They were not disappointed. He surged, his muscles held together, and he burst out with forty meters to go. The track nuts shouted, "I told you so! I told you so!" "Come on, Yerman! Come on!" "Show'em what you've got!" "There he goes! There he goes!"

Jack edged Earl Young by two-tenths of a second to win in 46.3.[71] Enthusiasts recorded Yerman as having run the two fastest consecutive 400 meters, the trials, and the finals, on the same day.[72]

The upset victory brought Margo running from the stands and onto the infield, where she hugged Jack and gave him a congratulatory kiss in front of sixty-five thousand spectators.[73*] Margo looked at the reporter and simply said, "I am so happy!" She already had her tickets to Rome and would leave the following week.[74]

The Sacramento Bee sportswriter captured the moment:

Big Surprise. Jack Yerman of Woodland, University of California senior, not only qualified for the

---

* Olympic Trials – Jack wins and Margo on the field:
  ▷ https://bit.ly/1960Trials

Olympic Games team, he upset the dope all over this huge stadium to win the 400-meter run.

Yerman gave up a promising football career to concentrate on track. He barely qualified for these final trials two weeks ago when he finished far back in the National Collegiate Athletic Association championships.

"I felt tired that day," said Yerman. "Today, I had it."

Asked how he trained for yesterday's race, Jack smiled and said: "I guess I didn't train at all. I just took it easy so I would have it when it counted. This was the race of my life."[75]

Jack (219) edges out Earl Young Olympic Trials

(Jack and Margo Yerman Collection)

The 1960 U.S. Olympic track team was the strongest and the strangest group of athletes. Wacky pole-vaulter Don Bragg hoped to be Hollywood's next Tarzan. The charismatic athlete had cleared fifteen feet nine and a quarter inches for a new world record and celebrated by thumping his chest like a bull ape. This brought "Jane" racing out of the stands into the ample arms of her beloved jungle fiancé. They both danced before Don signed hundreds of autographs: *"Tarzan Bragg."*[76]

Tom Murphy made the Olympic team by winning the 800-meter run and throwing up as he always did; Lieutenant George Young, the winner of the 3,000-meter steeplechase, where athletes jump over barriers and almost clear the water hazard on the other side, would be going to Rome. George had never seen the event until a year earlier when he surmised that this was something he could do. George had practiced for hours jumping over bales of hay at his ranch in New Mexico until he had mastered the art of the steeplechase.

Bill Nieder was a big disappointment at the meet. The mountainous man had gone back and forth with Olympian Parry O'Brien over the past year for world records in the shot put. Bill held the current record at sixty-five feet seven inches. The U.S. coaches had planned on stacking the team with Nieder and O'Brien, but Nieder injured his leg and failed to qualify. The coaches awarded Bill the precarious status of "alternate." This was a meaningless position because no alternate had ever been promoted. The U.S. Olympic Committee wanted Bill in the Games, and when Dave Davis, the athlete who made the team, injured his hand while lifting weights, the Olympic fathers unloaded Davis in favor of Nieder. The move confirmed a clear message to the rest of the team: "If you are injured, sick, or falter, do not let it be known." Jack had injured his knee in the 400 victory. If the coaches found out, he might be replaced. Jack trained for three days, the pain intensified, and he rested for two.

The Olympic team held practice meets in Eugene, L.A., the Bay Area, and shattered several world records; at their meet in Walnut, California, Jack anchored the mile relay against another set of Olympians. He came from behind to beat Glenn Davis, the world-record holder in the 400-meter hurdles. Jack's foursome set a new American and world record in 3:05.2.

It was time for Europe. The United States Olympic Committee loaded the U.S. track team onto a fleet of sluggish prop planes. In contrast, the U.S. officials traveled in luxurious jets. "Sending the team on the props saves money," they said, "and we need to arrive early to make arrangements." The officials' arrogant attitude would grow into a series of errors that would cripple the greatest track team ever assembled.

Jack and Margo On Their Way to Rome
(AP Photo)

CHAPTER 10

The Olympics in Rome

When ideals are obscured in amateur sports, then comes the danger of an athletic injury to the character of the athlete.[77]

Coach Brutus Hamilton

When Jack was nine years old, and every summer until he turned fourteen, he signed up for the YMCA summer camp. A youth counselor, Don Bloom, befriended the small boy. As a teenager, Jack played basketball and ping pong at the Y Center in town where Don worked. Don became the sportswriter for the *Woodland Daily Democrat* and eventually reported for *The Sacramento Bee* in the state's capital. Don, who had promoted Jack in the press, took it upon himself to raise funds to send Jack's mother to the Olympics in Rome.

Local Drive at $728. Every day it becomes more evident that Woodland is a pretty doggone nice place to live.

Community spirit our little city does not lack. Yesterday another local club and 14 individuals added $116 to "Send Mrs. Yerman to the Olympics" drive. These donations pushed the fund total up to $728 and really opened the door to achieving the goal of $1,300.

The drive is now .562 percent complete. It is picking up at an even faster tempo than earlier in the week. Daily totals have gone from $317 to $438 to $511 to $612 to $728.

If you aren't one of the 54 individuals or a member of one of the five clubs who have joined the campaign, you are more than welcome to send your donation to "Democrat Olympic Tour c/o Mrs. Yerman." I guarantee you'll sleep easier when you realize you've added to a most worthwhile local drive.[78]

The list of contributors grew, and the money poured in. The woman who worked nights, who never owned a car, who had never taken a vacation, joined a group of eighteen from Woodland and traveled to Rome to see Jack compete.[79] Irene kept a meticulous journal throughout the trip. She noted particulars that would seem mundane to experienced travelers, but the small details were an adventure for her. She kept a list of what she ate, the color of the blankets in the hotel, the shape of the bathtub faucets, the temperature of the water, the oxygen panels above the seats in the airplane, and what time the sun set:

August 29th, 1960. Luggage wgt. 34 lbs. Entered plane directly from airport. Pretty stewardesses. Canteens for workers at airport. 8:45 on our way. No room under seats for flight bags. 9:30 a.m. over Nevada; 10 a.m. coffee, coffee cake; 10:15 a.m. Salt Lake. Nebraska? Platte River? 12 noon Lunch — Tomato, seafood salad-peas, brown stew —peach with crumbs, graham cracker? Whipped cream—coffee; corn with rice....

Jack traveled with the American track team from New York to Switzerland on a chartered prop plane. The rested officials had arrived earlier in modern jets and greeted the weary-eyed athletes who unfolded themselves from their cramped conditions. The officials whisked the Olympians to a warm-up meet that afternoon. The team rested only a short night before boarding a train for a fourteen-hour journey to Rome and the historic Olympic Games.

The Olympics were born in ancient Greece, 776 BC, from a single foot-race near the banks of the Alpheus River at Olympia. The priests presented the champion, Coroebus, with a wreath of wild olive leaves woven from the twigs of a tree that Hercules had planted in the sacred grove near the Temple of Zeus. The Olympic Games were a religious event, honoring the gods through perfection — the perfect body of an athlete in sport. The Greeks hailed their Olympic heroes as idols in life and revered them as gods in death. All competitors had to declare that they were freeborn Greeks without taint or suspicion of sacrilege against their gods.[80]

Boxing, wrestling, chariot racing, and the marathon were added over the centuries to the original 200-meter footrace. An Olympic stadium was built that held nearly fifty-thousand spectators. Men competed without clothing. Women were not allowed to attend the Games until the mother of Pisidorus, a winning athlete, was discovered in the stadium watching her son. Pisidorus's mother had become his trainer when her husband died. She attended her son's race in disguise but could not contain herself when he won. Death was the penalty for such a crime, with victims thrown off a nearby cliff. In this case, the judges deemed the mother's cause honorable and spared her life. Women eventually participated in the Games, and Belisiche, a woman from Macedonia, won the chariot race in the 128th Olympic Games.

Scandal crept into the growing games. Theagenes, a priest of Hercules and all-around boxing champion, was disqualified when he cheated during a match. Upon his eventual death, the townspeople honored their local hero with a statue. One night, a jealous rival, who had never defeated the great

Theagenes, pushed the bronze likeness over. It wobbled in the wrong direction and fell, crushing the angry man. Another boxer killed his opponent in a final bout through a deliberate trick. The judges disgraced the athlete and gave the victor's crown to the dead man. Boxing scandals continued in the 98th Olympic Games. Eupolus of Thessaly bribed three opponents to let him win. He was discovered, disgraced, and fined. But the most significant punishment for him and others who violated the Olympic code was to be immortalized in statues called *Zanes*.[81] Their frozen images were carved in marble and placed at the entrance of the Olympic stadium with captions warning all athletes to remain steadfast and faithful to the religious and competitive spirit associated with the Games. Our word *zany* is derived from these dishonorable symbols.

The Games lost their religious significance over time as athletes sought gifts and money rather than respect and the gods' sacred olive wreath. Greece faded before the grandeur of Rome, and the Olympics lost their importance. The Romans held competitions from time to time until Emperor Theodosius I terminated the games by decree in 394. Barbarian invaders would pillage the Olympic temples. A century later, earthquakes completed the destruction, changing the course of the Alpheus River to rise and bury the hallowed plain where the first event had been run.

The 1960 Olympics returned to Rome after a 1,500-year absence. Rome had a millennium to prepare for the resurrection, and there would never be a venue so beautiful. The marathon ended in the shadows of the ancient Coliseum under the Arch of Constantine. The gymnastics competition took place in the ruins of the Baths of Caracalla, and wrestling was staged amid the visages of the once imposing Basilica of Maxentius. This was a beautiful city where centuries joined to contribute to the backdrop of the largest and most celebrated Games to date. Jack Yerman, a young man from a small town in California, stood in Rome to witness the convergence of history, architecture, and sports.

The Italians constructed *Villaggio Olimpico* for a record 7,725 athletes from eighty-seven nations.[82] It was a city within a city, complete with shopping centers, parks, play areas, landscaping, and a network of roads. The track and field events would be held in the modern Olympic Stadium that seated one-hundred-thousand spectators.

At a time when the United States was trying to make sense out of Jim Crow laws that sent Negros to the back of the bus and to separate drinking fountains, Rafer Johnson, Jack's teammate, all the more notable because he was black, carried the Stars and Stripes leading the red, white, and blue American team into the stadium. Each country traditionally dipped its flag as a tribute to the host nation when the delegation of athletes marched past the Tribune of Honor. Rafer did not dip his flag, and since the American colors did not drop, neither would the Russians lower their flag. The Soviet team marched into the stadium led by a square-jawed heavyweight who stiffly held the flagpole at arm's length.[83] The tensions between the two superpowers gave way to the Olympic spirit when the flamboyant Italians entered the stadium to an enthusiastic crowd. The Olympics had returned to Rome!

The Italians' flair for beauty and their contagious enthusiasm was evident everywhere. A reporter wrote of their fervent spirit at the twenty-kilometer racewalk finish line:

> **ROME, Sept. 4 (UPI)** Briton Stan Vickers swears the next time he finishes the 20-kilometer competitive walk, he'll remain upright, no matter how exhausted he is. After placing third in the Olympics, he laid down to rest. He was immediately seized by non-English-speaking ambulance men and rushed to a hospital on the outskirts of Rome. It took British officials several hours to find and "rescue" him.[84]

These Games were the first to be televised worldwide; new heroes emerged in the homes of everyday Americans. People in New York, Ohio, Wyoming, and California watched Wilma Rudolph sprint to gold. Wilma had suffered double pneumonia and scarlet fever as a child. She was number seventeen of nineteen children. She had been sickly and weak and wore a leg brace until she was eight years old. She discovered basketball, and her strength, coordination, and talents blossomed. Wilma set a high school state record, scoring forty-nine points in one game. She would go on to win three gold medals for the United States, running a fast 11.0 seconds in the 100-meter sprint and 24.0 in the 200-meter sprint. She anchored the 4x100-meter relay for an easy world record. [85]

The most historic event in the modern Olympics is the men's marathon, dating back to 490 BC. That was the year the Greek General Miltiades led nine thousand Athenians and a thousand allies to meet an even greater army of Persians near the city of Marathon. The Greeks fought for their wives, their children, and their country and pushed the fleeing Persians back to the sea. During the battle, the elders gathered in the Athens market to await news of whether their city would be safe or destroyed. Miltiades summoned a messenger, Pheidippides, to carry the news of victory. Pheidippides had fought through the torridity of battle. He tossed his shield aside, stripped himself of his armor, and sprinted for Athens. Inspired by the good news, and despite weary muscles, parched lips, and overwhelming fatigue, he raced the 26.2 miles, arriving exhausted and staggering into the city. At the feet of the elders and deathly short of breath, he delivered his message: "Rejoice; we conquer!" Pheidippides fell to the ground, gasped for air, and died. [86]

Years later, when Jack recounted his experience of the 1960 Games, he shared the story of the marathon runner who became a legend for his outstanding performance and his abilities to overcome adversity. The five-foot nine-inch, 128-pound Ethiopian shepherd, Abebe Bikila, who turned down an offer of shoes, ran barefoot over Rome's pavement and cobblestone streets through the night while Italian soldiers held torches to light the way. Bikila won in a record time of two hours, fifteen minutes, and seventeen seconds and became Africa's first black Olympic medalist and a national hero in his homeland. Emperor Haile Salassie promoted Bikila to the rank of captain of the Ethiopian Imperial Guard.

Bikila ran the 1964 marathon in Tokyo, but this time he wore shoes. Notwithstanding an emergency appendectomy a month before, he surpassed his previous record by more than three minutes. He finished the race by performing jumping jacks to show the crowd that he could have run further.[87] In the 1968 Mexico City Olympics, Bikila would leave the marathon after seventeen kilometers. His coach reported that Bikila had suffered a bone fracture in his left leg several weeks before and had not wanted it known.

Bikila's life unexpectedly changed in 1969. He was critically injured in an auto accident, and after months in the hospital and numerous spinal operations, he resigned himself to a wheelchair. Bikila said of his accident, "Men of success meet with tragedy. It was the will of God that I won the Olympics, and it was the will of God that I met with my accident. I accepted those victories as I accept this tragedy. I have to accept both circumstances as facts of life and live happily." [88] Bikila took up archery and competed in the Paraplegic Games. He died in 1973 at the age of forty-one from a brain hemorrhage. News of his death shocked the world, but his legacy lives as Africans continue to compete and win in his shadow.

Expectations for the "greatest American track team ever assembled" were high, but the team performed poorly in the Olympic heats; and in contrast to the hoopla before the trip, the Americans received a whiplash of negative press. Headlines read:

American Trackmen "Choked-Up" Say Russians

ROME, Sept 4 (AP) "...The Greatest danger for any sportsman is to be afraid," Litovev (coach of the Soviet hurdlers) said in an exclusive interview tonight. The Americans came here expecting to defeat everyone. When they found they could not do it, they became afraid.[89]

The world could only guess why the Americans fell short. Percy Cerutty, Australia's eccentric distance coach, speculated, "I don't think the Americans expected this heat. It has hurt the Australians as well." [90]

The record-breaking temperatures and high humidity played a role in the track team's demise. Still, it was not nearly so significant as the anxiety the American officials imposed upon the team. The prop plane, the quick warm-up meet, the long train ride, and foul water sapped the Americans of their strength and gave way to dysentery. Jack, like so many others, had trouble keeping liquids in his system. He was sick, but he did not dare share his condition with those who could administer medication. He and the others were afraid that they would lose their places on the team if they showed weakness as Dave Davis had after the Stanford trials. Jack's California teammate and close friend, Jerry Siebert, ran the 800-meter semifinals with a 101-degree fever and diarrhea. He was eliminated. The press vilified sprinter Ray Norton who ran out of his zone during the 4x400 finals, but he, like many on the team, was far from top form. [91]

Meanwhile, newspapers back home reported that the Americans were disloyal to their country, [92] passing the time with "wine, women, and song." [93] Coach Hamilton, sitting in Berkeley, read the reports and later quipped, "I knew all along that the claims were untrue. Jack and Jerry can't sing worth a lick."

Journalists tried various methods of entering the Olympic Village to speak with the team. One male sportswriter, dressed like a female athlete, was discovered and tossed out. [94] Don Bloom knew he needed to speak with Jack and attempted to enter the front gates, but the guards, with hands-on guns, stared him down, so he found another way. Outside, Don ran into "Mutt and Jeff" of the USC track team — little Max Truex at 5 feet 5 inches and 128 pounds and the American record holder in the 10,000 meters, and gigantic Rink Babka at 6 feet 5 inches, 267 pounds, who had won silver in the discus. Don told them how badly he needed to get into the Olympic Village.

"Don't worry about the security," Babka told Bloom, "Put on these ID pins. Athletes wear them to get in and out of the gate."[95] Don pinned the pass on his lapel and gave his wife the other pin. He lifted his chin, stood tall, and pulled the shoulders of his slight build back. His wife said he looked like a fencer, and she pretended to be a gymnast. They walked through the gates with a group of athletes, and inside they nearly stepped on Jack before recognizing him. Jack's cheeks had sunk, his complexion yellowed, and he walked head down, running into Don. He was very sick.

"It's great to see someone from home —" Jack's voice cracked.

"What's the matter with you? You're so thin," asked Don,

"I've lost fifteen pounds. I felt strong in Pomona, but the trip has been hard." Jack told Don the team was drained of strength, and his knee was swollen. "I'm afraid if they find out," said Jack, "they won't let me run. We're all sick from the food and water. The Russians were smart," continued Jack. "They brought their own water, and none of them is sick."[96] Jack's spirits lifted after talking to someone from home.

Jack won his first two heats in 47.2 and 46.4, but the illness prevailed, and he finished last in the semifinals at 48.9,[97] a second slower than he had run four years earlier as a high school senior. It took all of Jack's strength to finish the race far behind the others. The 400 was over for him. He dragged his dehydrated body back to the Village — to escape the people, the hot weather, and his disappointment in sleep.

Ticket to Olympic Stadium
(Used with Permission, IOC)

Don's Woodland group had traveled six thousand miles to see Jack win a gold medal. Jack had one more chance: the 1,600-meter relay, the final event of the Olympics. Would the American officials replace him? Years later, in his book Confessions of a Sportswriter, Bloom recalled the race:

No, because Coach Larry Snyder knew Jack's reputation for being more outstanding as a relay runner than when he was running for himself only. He was named to run the first leg in the race in which either the U.S. or Germany would have to break the world record to win. With him were 400-meter champion Otis Davis, sixth-placer Young, and Glenn Davis, who had won his second Olympic 400-meter hurdles title. Germany boasted 400-meter silver medalist Carl Kauffman, fifth-placer Manfred Kinder, and two more excellent one-lappers in Hans Reske and Johannes Kaiser.

When Jack got into his starting blocks, I felt more nervous than he appeared. Looking through binoculars at the man I coun-seled when he was a youngster at YMCA camp before becoming

121

an internationally known athlete, I could see he was far from being in peak physical shape. I had known him since he was a shy boy growing up in a broken home, was dedicated to his mother, and determined to better himself in scholastics and athletics. In his eyes, I saw that burning desire that made him the only man to compete in the Rose Bowl, Olympic Games, and Pan American Games. He deserved a gold medal. I said a quick, silent prayer.

At the gun, Yerman sprinted into the first turn like a man possessed by the devil. He had the spark. Running against Reske, he sped around the track as if it were the last race of his life. When an obviously exhausted Yerman handed the baton to Young, Uncle Sam's team was seven yards ahead of fourth-place Germany. Yerman's time was 46.2, the fastest opening lap in Olympic history. America went on to win a world record in 3:02.2 to Germany's 3:02.7. In my mind, that half-second margin was because of Yerman, but of course, I was slightly prejudiced.

Mrs. Yerman was even more proud as she stood tall when the giant scoreboard flashed the names of the American team; the foursome walked to the top of the victory stand, and the national anthem was played in their honor. With Margo Brown, who would become his wife, also in the stands, Yerman wore a wide smile as Old Glory was raised. He came — and he conquered. It was a race and a day I'll never forget.

I often wondered what it would be like to stand at the top of the victory stand. Several years later Yerman explained, "There are some similar highs. It's a combination of what you feel with the birth of your first son, college graduation, getting married and coming home after years of absence. When the flag is raised and the anthem is played, there is a bond that exists between the crowd and the athletes. This bond is as if everyone, for a brief moment, is a member of the nation of mankind. [98]

Irene sat in the stands wearing her new sunglasses and taking in the sights and sounds of the victory. She recorded the day and the event in her journal:

Sept. 8, 1960: Afternoon meet — cloudy. Hotel Michelangelo — luxury! English speaking people. Visited fruit and vegetable market — shops. Javelin throw — women's high jump. 1600 Meter Relay: threatening rain. Put on rain gear — hoping it wouldn't pour, at least until race over — no one left — sprinkling. Gold medal, whole stadium on their feet.

World Record Olympic 4x400 Team, left to right –
Earl Young, Otis Davis, Glenn Davis, and Jack Yerman
(AP Photo)

In the glow of the win and with gleaming gold medals around their necks, the four champions walked out of the stadium to a small warm-up field.* The men stood together and received congratulations from coaches, trainers, and fellow athletes. An Italian photographer, one of the infamous paparazzi, moved in and asked handsome Earl Young, the youngest of the four, to hold something. Earl instinctively received the object when, without warning, little Coach Eastman leaped forward and hit Earl like a linebacker. The object flew from Earl's hands and crashed to the ground, releasing the acerbic smell of strong alcohol. There, at his feet, lay a shattered bottle of whiskey. Jack realized that if the staged photo had been taken, it would have appeared in newspapers worldwide, where many were willing to believe that frivolous parties were the reason for the team's poor performance. The Americans were only a camera flash away from a scandalous photo and a cunning caption that might have read: Earl Young, USA Olympic Gold Medal Winner, Celebrates.

The Games ended with the United States' thirty-four gold medals to Russia's forty-three. The United States Olympic Committee president, Avery Brundage, charged the athletes with "getting too soft and complacent," and the cry of "wine, women, and song" was shouted again.[99] When Jack looked around the Olympic venue, he imagined a statue of the duplicitous American officials immortalized, like the Zane statues of old, for dishonoring the Olympic spirit.

---

* 1960 Olympic 4x400 Finals. Jack in lane three runs first leg:
  http://bit.ly/4x400Final1960

CHAPTER 11

Jack Yerman Day

You are headed for some amazing performances, and they will come soon and bring great pleasure to your many friends in Woodland as well as to your teammates and coaches here. Just carry on with the same determined enthusiastic attitude you had this season and things will work out.[100]

Coach Brutus Hamilton

When Jack told his roommate, Jim Ring, that he would be taking Margo to Woodland on the Greyhound bus to a parade in his honor, Jim replied, "Yerman, you gotta go in style. You're driving my new Corvette!" Jack did not argue.

The clear California autumn morning had begun to warm. Jack drove with the convertible top down, pushed his foot on the accelerator, and felt the horsepower surge within the little red Corvette. Margo's dark hair fluttered as they drove east on Interstate 80 from the Bay Area towards the city of Davis. The betrothed couple had dated for three years without owning a car and was happy for the rare occasion of riding alone. Margo's engagement ring sparkled from her hand; she would not wear it publicly until the engagement party held in their honor that evening in Woodland.

All of Woodland had followed Jack to the Olympics. Now, children ran a little faster, the high school football team practiced a little harder, and the Leithold Drug Store seemed a little busier. Mayor Frank Heard proclaimed this day, the twenty-first of October, as Jack Yerman Day:

WHEREAS, Jack Yerman has given outstanding service in sporting activities to Woodland High School and the City of Woodland;

WHEREAS, Jack Yerman has made similar accomplishments as a member of the University of California Track Team; and

WHEREAS, Jack Yerman did win a position on the United States Olympic Team; and

WHEREAS, Jack Yerman brought great acclaim to himself, his country, his school, and his home town as a member of the winning 1600-meter relay team in the Summer Olympics at Rome, 1960; and

WHEREAS, The City of Woodland is extremely proud of its Olympic Gold Medal winner and wishes to pay all tributes possible;

NOW THEREFORE BE IT RESOLVED that the City Council of Woodland, California, does hereby proclaim Friday, October 21, 1960, as "Jack Yerman Day" through the City of Woodland and does urge all Woodland citizens to join in the salute to Jack Yerman.

PASSED AND APPROVED by the Woodland City Council this 17th day of October, 1960.

Frank E. Heard Mayor, City of Woodland [101]

Jack turned off I-80 onto 99 North to Woodland. The car glided over the two-lane highway that separated fragrant peach orchards and earthy sugar beet fields. Mesmerized by the warming day and cadenced patterns of the agricultural rows, Margo's mind wandered back to the remarkable events of that summer:

TICKETS HERE!

"JACK YERMAN DAY"

Community Salute

Noon - Friday, Oct. 21st

Posted in Woodland

(Jack and Margo Yerman Collection)

Jack handed Margo a fistful of wadded bills before she left for Europe. "I've been to Europe before," he said, "and I know you can always use the extra money. Take a ride to the top of the mountain or do something special." They had talked of marriage, and Margo understood the request.

Margo traveled with Babs Feiling, her close friend and former college roommate. When the girls toured Amsterdam, the diamond capital of the world, it seemed a natural place to look for a ring. Margo window-shopped jewelry stores until she spied a petite .18 karat gold, *single band, with a .21 carat offset diamond. The thought of the ring brought her back to the window several times. She tried it on. The gold band curled around her finger, and rather than forming a perfect loop, one end gently lay over the other, like a gold ribbon resting on her finger with a small, solitary diamond sparkling from the top. I'd rather have this than a ride to the top of a mountain, she thought. Later, Margo left Babs in an art museum and secretly bought the ring for 125 dollars.*

The girls timed their trip to arrive in Rome a week before the Olympics. Margo and Babs caught the attention of the Italian men; shopkeepers reached up and pinched their youthful faces, and men on public transportation could not keep their claws off the two beauties, leaving the young ladies fuming from the pinches and bruised bottoms. The guards at the Olympic Village, possibly concerned with making a good impression, assumed the girls, with their bobbed hair, were American swimmers and allowed them to enter. Margo visited Jack and his teammates, and when no one was looking, she handed a non-descript package containing the wedding ring to Jerry Siebert, who quietly passed it on to Jack.

Jack welcomed time with Margo. They cheered for the Greco Roman wrestlers in the ancient redbrick Baths of Caracalla. They attended an opera with live horses and a Roman chariot. They explored Rome's streets and found their way to the Trevi Fountain, where Neptune entered the city on a magnificent seashell pulled by massive horses, and like thousands before, they turned their backs to the water and tossed coins over their shoulders. Legend has it that by so doing, they would someday return to Rome.

Margo and Babs occasionally ate with American friends in the cafeteria designated for American, Canadian, and British athletes until an Italian official wised up to the ruse and, flanked by two security guards, made a beeline for the girls. He shook his finger at the imposters and, in broken English, demanded that the girls leave. Margo and Babs gathered their things and walked to the gate. (Later, when the rumors of "wine, women, and song" surfaced, Margo believed the Italian official assumed she and Babs were prostitutes).

Immediately following the Olympic Games, the men's track team flew to Athens to compete in an exhibition meet. Margo, who had minored in Latin in Berkeley and was well-versed in Roman and Greek mythology, welcomed the offer to join the team in Athens if she could get herself there. The night after the 4x400 victory, Margo headed to Greece, where she would meet Jack, and booked a closet-sized room in the basement of the same hotel where the American team would stay.

Jack arrived with the team in Athens the next day, and the young couple ate dinner at a small rooftop restaurant. The warm night carried their conversation while a violin played in the corner. They ordered dolma, the traditional small bundle of spicy meat and rice wrapped in sweet grape leaves. After dinner, they strolled to the Temple of Zeus with its majestic columns. Jack pulled the ring from his pocket and turned to Margo. He held her hands and asked, "Will you marry me?"

Her eyes sparkled, and she said, "Yes!" They kissed. The next day they purchased a watercolor of the ruins of the Temple of Zeus from a street artist as a keepsake.

Turning the Corvette onto Woodland's Main Street brought Margo back to the moment. Margo removed her ring and slipped it into her purse. The champion had arrived in his chariot with his damsel by his side. Just as at the end of an Olympic race, when the athlete jogs around the track in victory, it was Woodland's turn to celebrate.

Jack returned to his home a Collegiate and AAU All American, the United States 400-meter champion, and a world-record holder. This was the most spectacular athletic career ever accomplished by a Woodland High School graduate. Jack was the only athlete in U.S. history to compete in the Olympic Games, the Pan American Games, and the Rose Bowl, and the only trackman in the world to run on teams that set world records in the mile, two-mile, and 1,600-meter relay events. Moreover, he ran with the University of California team that clocked the fastest ever sprint medley relay and was one of a few athletes to compete against the Soviets in the USSR.[102]

Jack gratefully acknowledged his hometown at the luncheon hosted by the Woodland Chamber of Commerce:

Woodland has a fine tradition of friendship, and I'll always be grateful. The highest honor I've ever received came from the people of Woodland. This came to me when you sent my mother to Rome to see me compete in the Olympic Games. This was the high point in both our lives, and we'll forever be grateful. I wish I could personally thank everyone who has helped us.

Jack paused for a moment and looked down the guest table to his mother. The handkerchiefs came out in every corner of the room when he said:

I especially want to thank my mother — for being my mother. You've always stood by me from the beginning and especially on a bad day.[103]

There would be more speeches, and half of the city's population lined the streets to wave to Jack, who led 103 entries in the largest homecoming parade to date. Jack's classmate and friend, Pat Welty, in charge of the Class of '56 float, stood proudly on the decorated truck bed, wearing Jack's dark blue Olympic sweats and holding an Olympic torch. After the parade, Woodland High held a pep rally and the homecoming football game.

Bill and Bethel Griffith invited guests to their home for a celebratory dinner before the night's big game. Visitors arrived at a sign Bethel had posted on the front door that read, "Jack and Margo, A Winning Team!" Inside, flickers of light bounced from Margo's engagement ring, surpassed only by her radiant smile. Irene, Jack's mother, sat off to one side of the room, still in wonderment at the far-off places she had seen and the thrill of her son's successes. Jack's sister, Kathy, cheerful as ever, laughed and talked easily with friends. Margo's sister, Karen, who had driven from her desert home in Taft to represent Margo's parents, chatted with fellow Taftian, Jan Smith, a *Cal* song leader, and Margo's dear friend. Well-wishers include Don Bloom, the sportswriter and years earlier young Jack's YMCA counselor, and Bob Griffith, Bill's brother, who just a few years ago had interviewed the eager boy at the drug store, and Coach Brutus Hamilton, who taught Jack life's lessons on the track and would continue his friendship for many years. Guests embraced the Olympian and his smart, spunky, and beautiful fiancé.

PART II

The Victory Lap

CHAPTER 12

Operation Yankee

No one of the thousands who saw or the millions who heard the Games but what was cleansed and ennobled in spirit because of it. Who knows, my dears? Who knows? Maybe the prophet Isaiah who said, "How fair upon the mountain are the feet of them that bring glad tidings." [104]

Coach Brutus Hamilton

Margo knew her parents did not approve of Jack. Bruce could be stern, opinionated, and weaponize the silent treatment; and, Della worried excessively. Margo wrote to her parents:

October 6, 1959

Dear Mother and Daddy,

Jack and I have talked for a long time about getting married, but there were always too many obstacles. The worst part of this is that we haven't spoken to you about it.

I know some of the things you're saying – I'm infatuated with an athlete. Brother, I can hardly wait 'til he stops running in circles. But so long as it gets him through school and to Europe, he'll continue. He doesn't have money – well, neither do a lot of couples.

No, Mother, Jack isn't handsome, but he's nice looking. And he's a heck of a lot healthier than I'll ever be. No, he's never had a close family life – but he wants to be as good a father as his friends' fathers were to him.

Yes, we're young and idealistic and don't know everything. We're not afraid to yell at each other, and we know there'll be plenty of times that are more bad than good...

Well, Mother and Daddy, I finally did it – what you've feared for 20 years, 11 months, and 14 days. It's not so bad after all, is it? Besides, he's getting some fine in-laws!

All my love, Margo [105]

Margo's mother was a member of the Church of Jesus Christ of Latter-day Saints, a Mormon, and her father was not, so living in a mixed-religion family was familiar to Margo. She admired Jack's resilience, intelligence, and humility, And he was funny! As she got to know him, she recognized he was also looking for a direction. He was shy and somewhat awkward in groups. His journey had been remarkable from childhood to here, and she wanted him to be happy. Jack graduated in January and reported to Fort Benning in Georgia for Basic Training. He and Margo wrote frequently:

Tomorrow is Sunday, darling. Please don't turn down the chance to try and find out more about the church if you get around some of those Utah or Idaho boys. Instead of just hearing, think carefully... I'm positive this is what you are looking for.[106]

They had talked about marriage, but it wasn't until April that he learned he would have a short leave in June. So, with a month to plan, Margo prepared for a full-scale wedding on June 4, 1961. They would be married in Taft, at

Margo's church, and Della's brother, Merlin, a Bishop in Los Angeles, would perform the wedding.

Frugality was an adventure for Margo, and the wedding was not immune from the penny-pinching. She found a sleeveless, off-the-shoulder, traditional wedding dress at a bridal shop in Oakland. It hugged her tiny waist with a wide girth of lace applique from top to bottom. She asked the price, "$17.00." She wrote to Jack, "My wedding dress is ugly. Glad it's the thought that counts!"

"She makes everything look good!" mused Jack.

Jack flew into Bakersfield on June 1. He was excited and maybe a little scared as Bruce drove him to Taft. Two days later, he met with a pair of 19-year-old boys in white shirts and ties to continue the missionary lessons he had started two years previously. They discussed the nature of God, and that God communicates with his children. The young men invited him to read from the Book of Mormon:

And when ye shall receive these things, I would exhort you that ye would ask God, the Eternal Father, in the name of Christ, if these things are not true; and if ye shall ask with a sincere heart, with real intent, having faith in Christ, he will manifest the truth of it unto you...[107]

Jack remembered the reassuring whispers he had heard as a child, "*Your time will come.*" Jack knew that God had been talking to him for a long time. His thoughts jumped back to his experience in the sorority date room when, as he prayed, he felt a powerful reassurance just before the young woman entered, surprising all, and he had bolted to his feet.

Jack looked at the two young men and said, "Let's do this," Jack became a member of the Church of Jesus Christ of Latter-day Saints on June 3, 1961. He was twenty-one years old and married Margo, his dark-eyed bride, the next day before 325 family and friends.

Margo Jo Brown Yerman

(Jack and Margo Yerman Collection)

The newlyweds settled into a small Berkeley apartment in July. Both had graduated in January, but Margo would attend summer school to finish her teaching credential while Jack fulfilled his Army obligation at the Presidio across the bay. Their first apartment was a small castle. The stove, refrigerator, and cabinets were in arm's length of each other, and the two-person dining table was a step away. The newlyweds emptied the freezer of its peas, ice cream, and meat each Wednesday before the building manager defrosted the centrally controlled iceboxes on Thursdays. Jack spent much of the year running for the Army around the world, while Margo taught as a substitute. In March of 1962, Margo learned she was pregnant.

Lieutenant Yerman received his army orders to report to Nuremberg, Germany, and train for the Conseil International du Sport Militaire (CISM), the military's version of the Olympics. Its motto: Friendship through sport! Its goal: to contribute to world peace by uniting armies through friendly competition. While the athletes competed for a week, Cold War diplomats met behind the scenes. Jack's assignment: a month of training in Germany, then report with the unit for the international competition in the Netherlands with twenty-one nations and a tour to Brussels following the meet. Athletes came from all military branches, and the NATO countries traditionally thumped the combat-waiting Americans. This time, the United States called up its hotshots to regain a little respect.

Lieutenant Jack Yerman

(Jack and Margo Yerman Collection)

Jack kissed Margo goodbye. Twelve American soldier-athletes met in London and headed for historic Nuremberg, the ancient Roman stronghold and a city that had witnessed massive Nazi rallies. The athletes stayed in the city center and traveled by Willy's jeep to the stadium that Hitler had used for the 1936 Olympics and Nazi rallies.

Jack anticipated easy workouts and would use off-hours for sightseeing, but the mission-focused Colonel barked out different plans. "Soldiers, you are here to win for the United States. You will report to the venue for training at 1030 hours and return to your quarters at 1500 hours. You are authorized to go to the stadium and must return to the hotel." The recruits complained, and the Colonel belted back, "This is important, and nothing will interfere with your success!"

"Well," mumbled the team…, "but after the meet, can we have some fun?"

"That would be permissible." The Colonel promised to timetable sight-seeing after the mission.

The team traveled eight hours by bus from Nuremberg, Germany, to Hertogenbosch in the Netherlands, more commonly known as The Duke's Forest in memory of its twelfth-century landlord. Like Nuremberg, it had escaped much of WWII's destruction, although it held a Nazi concentration camp of 30,000 prisoners.

The Americans dominated the meet, and Jack set a new record. The Colonel in charge puffed his chest a bit larger, he walked a bit lighter, and the corners of his mouth lifted from its perpetual frown. Stars and Stripes staff writer Dick Gitlin reported:

```
Yerman was credited with [Sunday's] only CISM
record — second of the meet plus one tied mark —
when he knocked four-tenths of a second off the 400-
meter standard with a 46.5 effort. The anchorman
on Saturday's record-setting 1,600-meter relay
quartet, Yerman eclipsed a record he had equaled
last year while taking the metric quarter mile in
Brussels.[108]
```

Lieutenant Yerman
Wearing CISM Warm-ups
(Jack and Margo Yerman Collection)

The team organized its gear, boarded the bus, and bounced down the road on high hopes for some free time in Brussels before flying back to the States.

"Hey, Colonel, this is the wrong way!" yelled one of the men.

The Colonel said nothing.

"Colonel, where are we going?"

"All I can say is that you are going on the most important mission of your lives…" Jack felt the bus hit a pothole.

"What does that mean?"

"That's all you need to know. You will be told more when we are airborne."

Jack's brows narrowed, "Airborne?" He had no way of communicating with Margo and slumped back in his seat.

They drove through the Netherland countryside's late afternoon shadows, passing dairy farms dotted with mounds of drying hay. The bus rounded a turn, and the team spied an aircraft parked behind a large barn, a classic World War II DC-3 transport plane that had never returned from Europe. The Colonel ordered each to grab his gear to board the rumbling aircraft. Jack felt the engines reverberate, their exhaust tickling his nose. He approached the steps behind the wing to find a bench seat. He sat under the bare metallic walls near the door of the curved fuselage. The pilot looked back from the cockpit, "Good evening, men. Stow your bags, put on a parachute, and welcome aboard!"

Parachutes? Few of them had seen a parachute up close, and before one could assimilate the new surroundings, the complexity of straps, and where to put his bags, the plane accelerated down the grass runway and lifted into the dusk.

The men pressed the Colonel for more information.

"I am not authorized to divulge information before landing."

Looking out the windows, they saw lights of villages drift by but could not tell which direction they flew. An hour and a half later, the plane circled a large city, descended, hit the tarmac, and coasted to a halt near an Army staff car obscured in the shadows of night. The athletes disembarked. Their eyes widened and adjusted as they made out the brass of six Army "Bird Colonels."

"Where are we? What's going on?"

The men were ordered onto a bus, which drove them to the middle of an adjacent airstrip. The German driver disembarked and walked a hundred meters distant from the group. The athletes sat in the dark for ten minutes until the headlights of a jeep sped across the runway towards them. The vehicle halted, and Major Balk boarded the bus. He wore dark sunglasses at night and held a legal-size manila envelope. Jack made out the wax seal of a shield and two swords of the Joint Chiefs of Staff. He noted the red letters stamped across the envelope, "Top Secret."

The Major blew cigar smoke into the air and looked over the group. "Men, I am your briefing officer for 'Operation Yankee.'" The Major pried open the envelope and looked up to the men, "This is a secret military exercise, and if you speak of this in the next ten years, you will be sentenced and convicted to Leavenworth's Federal Penitentiary." He barked, "Now, Operation Yankee! Your orders, men!"

Jack remembers the information like this: "You will depart at 22:30 hours for Heidelberg, where you are part of a program to entertain Field Marshall and Russian General Ivan I. Yakubovsky..."

Yakubovsky was the Russian hero who had defeated the Germans in the Battle of Berlin almost two decades earlier. Later, Stalin exiled him to Siberia, but recently, Khrushchev brought him back into Soviet graces as Commander of the million-man Russian Army in East Germany.

This would be the Field Marshall's first trip to the West, and the track team, who happened to be in the neighborhood, was entertainment to keep him from seeing anything significant. The Army planned a three-hour demonstration at the Heidelberg soccer stadium where he would watch martial arts, parachuting, an exhibition of American football, bow shooting, a track meet, and an 80-member all-Army band.

The terse battle orders continued, "The 400 meters will be run. Lieutenant Dunkelberg will take the lead for the first 200 meters, and Lieutenant Cassel will pass him. Then, Lieutenant Yerman will pass Lieutenant Cassel and win the race in a time of 44.9."

44.9 would match the world record.[109] Jack protested, "Sir, I can't run that fast."

He cut Yerman short, "Follow orders, Lieutenant!"

"Yes, sir." Now, all understood that this was a military operation.

After the briefing, the driver returned and took "Operation Yankee" to the barracks. The athletes asked the Army to alert their families that homecoming would be delayed for two weeks. Margo was approaching her third trimester, and Jack wanted to know how she was doing. Request denied. This event would be off the radar.

In the morning, the weary track unit reported to an oval scratched out of a soccer field. Jack looked at the rutted lanes and remembered some of the rural high school tracks he'd run on back home. *The General is not stupid*, he mused. *He'll know we can't run world-class times on this track.* Jack mustered the courage to speak to the Colonel, "Sir, I can't run on that track."

"It will be fixed, Lieutenant."

The Army Corps of Engineers left in the middle of the night, pulling heavy equipment behind large trucks. Two days later, the caravan crawled back loaded with tons of red volcanic cinders from an Italian volcano hundreds of miles to the south. Teams of soldiers unloaded the tiny gravel onto the oval and groomed the track into a shiny, smooth surface. Jack stepped onto the new track. He accelerated from a jog to a run, and the red dust lifted from his heels, leaving a path of divots in the wake. "This won't do," he said, and the Army worked on a plan to harden the track.

The theatrics in Heidelberg continued, but the Army's directors kept the script to themselves, and the actor-athletes protested with a half-hearted effort. The stage was in poor condition, information was scarce, and the men grumbled. The simmering came to a boil when a four-star general grabbed the microphone and shrieked for order and discipline on the field. He warned that any communication with home would be a violation of security. The Olympic 800 runner from the Airforce, Ernie Cunliffe, pulled a muscle and limped around the track. Years later, Ernie revealed he had faked the injury.

Meanwhile, back home, Jack had not returned as planned. Margo contacted the Presidio in San Francisco, "We don't know where he is…," Undaunted, Margo telephoned the Pentagon in Washington. "We don't know where he is either, but we will find out." They called Margo and apologized, "We can't find him."

Jack had disappeared! She invoked scenarios that did not end well. Had he been kidnapped? Did the Russians take him? Did his bus leave the road and disappear down a hidden ravine? Maybe he bumped his head and wandered off in a homeless fog of amnesia?

The day to entertain General Yakubovsky arrived. The performers and two thousand troops assigned to fill the stadium arrived three hours before the General's scheduled time. Jack needed to use a men's room and climbed down the back of the grandstands to look for the required venue. He could not find a bathroom, so a soccer dugout would provide a fair substitute. He stepped into its shadows to be confronted by a man already there, "Where do you think you're going?"

Jack turned and looked down the barrel of an exotic automatic pistol in the hands of an American civilian dressed in a suit and a derby hat. Jack gulped, "Back to the stands, sir."

Yakubovsky's motorcade of five black Russian sedans crossed the Creuzburg Checkpoint shortly after 8 a.m. The General, accompanied by U.S. Army Major General James H. Polk, drove nearly three hours to Heidelberg and entered the tightly secured parade grounds lined with 200 US Army Honor Guards.[110] Yakubovsky, a solid man who stood a bit taller than most, exited his motorcade, saluted, and inspected the troops. His square jaw, cleft chin, thin lips, and penetrating eyes added to an aura of confidence. U.S. General Paul L. Freeman Jr. welcomed the Russian visitor.

Photo Jack snapped of Russian General
climbing bleachers to his seat

(Jack and Margo Yerman Collection)

Stars and Stripes, the American military newspaper, reported:

> The Russian, accompanied by four major generals of his staff, was accorded a 17-gun salute by six 105mm howitzers fired by the 8th Inf Div's salute batter from the 16th Army.
>
> As the smoke from the big guns cleared away, spectators saw that one of the Soviet Union flags which flew around the field had been blown to the ground by muzzle blast. The red flag with yellow sickle and hammer, however, was quickly picked up by American soldiers, and a new one run up. [111]

The show began with skydivers, followed by a special forces squad rappelling from helicopters, and the 8th Division's American football team played an abbreviated game while an interpreter explained the rules. [112] The track meet concluded the day, and the men staged the 400 as ordered: Lieutenant Dunkelberg took the lead for the first 200 with Lieutenant Cassel fighting for position and passing him. The crowd roared when Jack accelerated to overtake the runners and cross the tape in 46.6. [113] Jack had asked a teammate to keep the real-time: 48.2. *I hope the General left his stopwatch at home*, Jack muttered.

Jack thought to telephone Margo, but a call was not a real option for a soldier. [114] Jack would have to give contact information to a hotel clerk, who would connect to a local operator, who would link to the international operator of that country, who would connect to the international operator in the U.S., who would call a local operator, who would connect to Margo, who might not be home. The call would be expensive and with a good chance of error. He would be charged, regardless. [115*] Jack liked the idea of surprising Margo just the same.

---

* *A three-minute call, from Germany, at its best, could be $50.00 (the 1962 minimum wage: $1.15 and the average yearly salary $5,000).*

Margo awoke to a loud knock in the middle of the night. She pulled on her robe, unlocked the deadbolt, and cracked open the door to find Jack grinning on the other side. She reached out and hugged him, then stepping back and demanded, "Where have you been?"

"On a top-secret mission, and I cannot tell you more than that."

Margo's brows furrowed as she looked at him, "Really?"

Jack imagined hard labor and pounding rocks at Leavenworth for ten years, and then he thought of the next few days with Margo, and he melted. "Okay, I'll tell you everything…"

The papers across the U.S. reported the historic General's visit, and sports pages picked up on Jack's 400 win. "You sure caught a fast one in Heidelberg," a Berkeley fan commented.

"Yeah," Jack rolled his eyes. "It's nice to run for the Army."

CHAPTER 13

Out of Africa

My blessing upon the new little emigrant from Heaven who has come to live with you and upon his lovely mother and proud father. May he live long and prosper in all of life's True Values, and may his many fine achievements be a source of continuous joy and satisfaction to his good parents.[116]

Coach Brutus Hamilton

It seemed to Margo that Lieutenant Yerman had not been home long enough to unpack, but that mattered little to the Army and ordered Jack to Africa with the U.S. State Department to promote goodwill and provide track clinics to athletes on that continent. He would be gone for two months, returning in November. This would be Jack's third international trip for the State Department during their pregnancy. The baby was due near Thanksgiving. Margo packed her bags and caught the train to Bakersfield and then to her hometown in Taft to stay with her parents.

Jack would join seven other athletes and State Department officials for a tour that included Rhodesia, Kenya, Madagascar, Uganda, Egypt, Cyprus, Greece, and Israel. The group visited a location for a week, attending receptions and holding clinics. The soldier-athletes received no extra pay but were given an unlimited expense account. Jack often ordered a Chateaubriand, a three-inch-thick tenderloin steak cooked rare.

Jack called the experience magnificent. He wrote daily on tissue paper, which used fewer stamps, and "took a ballpoint really well." Margo typed the letters and shared them with Don Bloom, the Sports Editor for Woodland's Daily Democrat, who printed them in the local newspaper. Jack wrote with a perspective beyond his 23 years:

We are 11,000 miles from San Francisco's cool, damp fog. I expected to fly by prop to a remote landing field to meet a white hunter and pack our way through the jungle to meet the natives. Tarzan is not the only African myth. I discovered that my idea of Africa is also a myth so far as Southern Rhodesia is concerned. Salisbury, the capital, is one of the most modern cities I've seen. But it's a nation with severe social and political problems. Soldiers armed with submachine guns swarm the airport, and at the hotel, Arthur Cable, head of the United States Information Service, briefed us on the political situation. The government outlawed the ZAPU Peoples Party, the one-party that represented the black majority, and prior they had banned three similar parties.

This country has a race situation similar to apartheid of South Africa. The separation of races, resulting in segregation and political and economic discrimination against the non-Europeans, creates a situation where Africans live in a section of town with their own stores, clubs, schools, and local government. Our opening press conference was a strained affair. The white-minority Dutch control the government, military, and wealth. They dislike Americans because they feel we'd like to see the country go to the majority, the black Rhodesians. Unfortunately, the Federation has its eyes on the U.S.'s racial problems, which have never been anything to flaunt before the world.

We soon depart for Lusaka in Northern Rhodesia. It is the only place in the Federation where the black man is a social equal to the Dutch. I'm encouraged to learn that its University is mixed.[117]

Jack at Track Clinic in Cyprus
(Jack and Margo Yerman Collection)

The multi-country tour ended on the island of Cyprus, and Jack booked a ticket for home rather than join the team in Israel for an extended stay. Della, who had been taking care of Margo, wrote in her journal:

Jack was in Africa. His assignment was over, and he showed up at our home on November 10. I awoke in the morning to the front door closing. Margo's room was empty. I went out on the porch, looked down the street, and saw Margo and Jack in pajamas carrying a book on how to tell when the baby is due. They peered into it and walked again. They stopped, rechecked the book, and Jack put his arms around Margo. She was in labor! "Margo, it's time to go to the hospital!"

"The book doesn't say so," responded Margo.

Della, who worked in the billing office at the West Side District Hospital, grabbed the car keys. "Jack, let's go. Help Margo into the car." Jack assisted Margo into the Mercury's back seat, ran back into the house, and grabbed Margo's suitcase. The engine rumbled, and Della pulled the column shifter into first and then second gear. The white-knuckled soon-to-be grandmother drove her route to the red-tiled white stucco hospital on East North Street.

As Della shifted and accelerated around a corner, Jack said to Margo, "Do you remember the article I sent you on babies and cold milk?"

Margo had devoured literature on pregnancy and babies, and Jack contributed by sharing whatever he found. Margo sat reclined as much as possible in the back seat. "Yes, I read it."

Della maneuvered the car to the hospital's front door. Jack was told to wait in the lobby, and the nurses escorted Margo to the maternity ward. Dr. Ellis arrived, and Margo, in labor and on the table, was thinking of cold milk, "I've been reading that it is safe to give baby's cold milk."

"Hmmm," Dr. Ellis mumbled through the surgical mask.

Margo winced through a contraction. But as it was her nature to plan ahead, she continued, "Studies show there are no adverse effects."

"The idea seems entirely plausible," the doctor chuckled. "I wish my wife and I had tried it six children ago." He assured Margo the baby would be fine.

Della made her way to the delivery room to support her daughter, but her stomach knotted up when she heard Margo's cries.

I felt every pain Margo experienced. I covered the floor in tears and left for my office. I tried typing in my journal but could not concentrate. Dr. Ellis showed up after a long time, smiling and shaking his head, "I don't know why such small mothers have such big babies" Bruce

Hamilton Yerman was 22 inches and 9½ pounds, 2½ pounds bigger than predicted. "Margo and the baby are fine." As soon as we could drag Jack away from the nursery window, we went home. Jack immediately began making long-distance phone calls to his mother, friends, the Hamiltons, and the Griffiths.[118]

Bruce's first bottle at home and every bottle after would be cold. In a manifesto Margo submitted for publication, she shared:

```
I ignored the significance of the cold-milk theory
and rejoiced that Jack was concerned about his baby.
However, two national magazines issued the same story
in the next two weeks: Doctors at Bellevue Hospital
in New York City had fed newborns cold milk for two
years. Four years ago, a Texas doctor tried the same
experiment on 150 babies. They found no significant
differences between babies fed on warm or cold milk.[119]
```

Jack hoped to recreate his boyhood adventures with his children. They would play football and basketball, hike and camp, build forts, and make rubber-band guns. But he worried. He grew up during WWII and the Korean Conflict, and now school children practiced "duck and cover" drills, and U2 spy planes were shot down in Russia. Jack would lose friends in Vietnam and wonder if he could be called to duty or maybe his children would go to war. He kept these feelings to himself.

Jack's last official military assignment was to run in the 600 at the National AAU Championship in New York. Sports Illustrated reported:

```
Lieutenant Jack Yerman, on the eve of leaving the
Army, took the 600 in a strong closing rush, then
announced his retirement. [120]
```

Jack received his discharge in February of 1963.

CHAPTER 14

The Swiftest Man in A Business Suit

Many problems can be circumvented by anticipation... An educated man should be a civilized, adjustable animal.[121]

Coach Brutus Hamilton

Jack walked through the glass doors of a top Fortune 500 company's west coast complex to report to his second-floor corner office. "Hello, Jack " The security guard tipped his hat to *The Swiftest Man in a Business Suit*, as Jack was christened in the corporate magazine:

> Few employees know that they work alongside a former Olympic competitor. Although election to a United States team is a great tribute, our man distinguished himself even further... He won the highest athletic honor...A gold medal... His name is Jack Yerman. He is the supervisor of Personnel and Purchasing at our Menlo Park Plant...[122]

The three-page article highlighted his 1958 track tour behind the Iron Curtain, playing in the 1959 Rose Bowl against Iowa, his military service, running for the Army, and his 1962 diplomatic tour in Africa.

It was strange and exciting for Jack and Margo to settle down into a routine of commuting, shopping, taking care of a baby, and doing it all over again the next day. Jack did not miss the travel, and running was replaced by church basketball. The young couple moved their little family across the Bay to Santa Clara, where Margo found a job as an English teacher at the local high school. She hired Mrs. Ernborg, a stout, grey-haired German grandmother, to help at home and care for Bruce during the day. To calm the baby, Mrs. Ernborg mixed a sweet ambrosia of Karo syrup and water.

Jack and Margo's small apartment had no furniture. They ate dinner around a tablecloth spread on the floor. They planned to purchase a house, settle in the valley and make this location their home. Eventually, they found a home for sale on a quiet cul-de-sac.

The eager pair entered the bank's doors and were directed to an office with floor-to-ceiling glass on one wall and dark wood paneling throughout. The banker wore a dark wool suit with faint pinstriping. He extinguished the Lucky Strike cigarette in the ashtray and stood from his desk to greet them. First, he shook hands with Margo and then with Jack. Greying sideburns marked his clean-cut dark hair. "Please sit," he said, motioning to the chairs opposite his desk. The smoke from the smoldering cigarette tickled the noses of the young couple. "What can I do for you?" he asked.

"We've found a home," said Jack, "and we'd like to look at financing. They are asking $15,000 for the property." The banker's chair was turned slightly towards Jack, but he kept glancing at Margo. The man behind the desk inquired about Jack's salary. Jack responded that he made $650 a month and added, "Margo is teaching, and our combined salary is nearly $1,000 a month."

The banker looked at Jack, and his eyes darted for a moment to a poised Margo. "I'm sorry," he said, "but we cannot include Margo's salary. The net income of a family may only be considered if the wife is over 35, or if her doctor can produce a certificate that a young woman cannot bear children." [123]

Margo was attractive, smart, and confident. She had polish and presence from her years in debutante pageants and had been a finalist for Miss California. She had developed, organized, and managed the Student Publicity and Public Relations Office at the University of California, and when she graduated, they hired three people to replace her. She traveled the world, spoke Latin, earned a degree in English, graduated with distinction, and was a professional educator. Single women were not eligible for credit in the 1960s, and a married woman could only get a credit card if her husband cosigned. Except for Utah, which allowed women on juries in 1879, women were "too fragile to hear the grisly details of crimes and too sympathetic by nature to be able to remain objective." It wasn't until 1973 that women could serve on juries in all 50 states." Yale and Princeton would not accept female students until 1969, Harvard not until 1977, and "Brown, Dartmouth, and Columbia would not offer admission to women until 1971, 1972, and 1981, respectively." [124]

Margo looked the middle-aged man in the eyes and smiled to temper her direct question. "We both are working, we have childcare, we have a good, combined income, and you are telling us that we will not qualify for a loan?"

"I'm sorry," said the officer. "Maybe if you secure a larger down payment, we can make Jack's salary work, but at this time, there is nothing we can do."

Jack's shoulders drooped. They left the bank frustrated. Jack and Margo were equals in all. But, unfortunately, the financial institutions and much of the country were not moving at the pace Jack and Margo had become accustomed to with race or women. "This is not right," said Jack.

Jack escorted Bruce in his stroller for an early evening walk near their apartment and down Highland Avenue in Santa Clara. The rhythmic spaces in the sidewalk calmed the baby and left Jack pushing in silence. They turned a corner onto Roxbury, where Jack noticed an older man pushing a rotary lawnmower in the softening midsummer heat. The man maneuvered around a *For Sale* sign and greeted Jack with a "Hello" in a distinct German accent, and added some kind words about the baby.

"Is this your place," asked Jack, admiring the crisp paint, the square hedges, the manicured lawn.

"It is," said the man. "It's a fourplex – it has one three-bedroom unit, and the others are two bedrooms."

Jack had remembered a discussion he had with a fraternity roommate at *Cal*. "Hey, Yerman, never buy a house when you get married. Buy an apartment! You won't need to show your income to qualify. The rents have to cover the loan payments." Jack and Margo did the math, and with the help of Margo's father, as an investor, they were homeowners and landlords all at once, moving into the three-bedroom unit just before Thanksgiving. The payment from the tenants covered all expenses and they lived rent-free, bettering anything the bank could have offered.

CHAPTER 15

Comeback

When you see 20 or 30 men line up for a distance race in some meet, don't pity them... You are probably looking at the 20 or 30 best "bon vivants" in the world. They are completely and joyously happy in their simple tastes, their strong and well-conditioned bodies, and with the thrill of the wholesome competition before them... Their lives are fuller because of this competition, and their memories will be far richer. That's why men love to run. There is something clean and noble about it.[125]

Coach Brutus Hamilton

Margo met Jack at the door after work near the end of a gray California winter day in late 1964. "Do you have any running gear around the house?"

"Why?" Jack wondered.

"I heard on KGO radio that the U.S. indoor winners will be going to Europe for a series of meets," she smiled," and the wives go along! Do you think you could do this?"

Jack knew a "yes" was the only option. He walked to the bathroom scale and weighed himself. "175 pounds. That part's okay," he sighed. "I'll start training next week."

Margo suggested the sooner his training began, the better their chances. Jack started a routine the following morning and returned after work to run again at seven. He would train for two months and then run a time trial in early spring. After that, if he ran fast enough, he would enter an all-comers meet and compete in the track circuit. On a chosen day, Margo, Bruce, and Jack headed to the nearby high-school track. Jack stretched and warmed up with a few intervals. Margo held the stopwatch, and when Jack dropped his hand at the starting line, she hit the watch at the finish line: 220-yards in 22.5 seconds. "Excellent!" he exclaimed, and Margo smiled.

Jack entered the 220-yard sprint at a local all-comers meet. He felt confident, knelt at the starting blocks, the gun fired, and he sprinted to the curve, but the amateur field was with him — and passed him. "23.5 seconds." *What happened?* The following day, Jack returned to measure the practice track. "Hey, this track is only 400 yards!" He had run 20 yards short.

Jack ran a leg of the mile relay at the next meet. The paper reported:

```
Jack Yerman, a 1960 U.S. Olympian who hasn't run
outdoors for two years, posted a 48.00 quarter-mile
relay leg for the [San Jose] Youth Village.126
```

And two weeks later:

```
Making a comeback after a short retirement, Jack
Yerman won the 440-yard dash in 48.6.(127)
```

The current outdoor 440-yard sprint record stood at 44.9.[128] In Jack's prime, he was the fastest in the Pacific Coast Conference at 47.3,[129] and he had been clocked at a lightning 45.8 in a world-record-setting mile relay. Jack understood he had to work harder than anyone in the country to be ready for the Indoor National Championships. He laced his army boots, placed 60 punishing pounds of sand in his Army pack, and wiped his eyes. Jack faced the chosen 300-yard hill in a gravel quarry outside of town.[130] The first run up the slope, he felt good. The second, the third, and the fourth, his legs groaned under the weight of the backpack as he lifted his boots up the mountain. Jack kept pushing, and after a few weeks, the strength, power, and speed returned to his legs. He took the sand off his back, put on his spikes, and he flew! Jack ran against the nation's best and won in San Francisco and Los Angeles. He was ready for New York's Madison Square Garden.

Jack had little money. Don Bowden, his former *Cal* teammate and the first American to run the mile under four minutes, had developed the "Citius 4," a new track shoe that Jack was testing,[131] but Jack needed transportation across the country. Jack had won the 600 at the meet and set an American Record two years prior. He called the meet directors as a returning champion, and they sent him a plane ticket.*

American Record Certificate 600, 1963

(Jack and Margo Yerman Collection)

---

* Jack wins at Philadelphia Inquirer Games in 1961:
   ▶ https://bit.ly/JackInquirer

The officials gathered to finalize details on Thursday evening before the Friday night heats. Athletes did not attend these meetings, but Jack was there advocating that runners advance to the finals by winning a heat and not by overall time. If not, a single fast heat could advance all its runners leaving the top finishers from other heats in the stands. Jack ran strategically, maybe the best indoor runner in the country, and experience was his advantage. The officials agreed to seed the finals by heat winners rather than by time.

Indoor tracks are made of wood and vary in size. All are short, and the Garden track was a tight 160 yards around with banked turns. The outer lane on the curve stood several feet higher than the inside lane, and sprinters leaned on the centripetal forces to keep them from flying off the track.

The first 600-yard heat featured 1960 gold medalist Jack Yerman and Mike Larrabee, the 1964 400-meter gold medalist. Jack, on the outside lane, was determined to beat the runners to the curve. The gun fired, and an anxious Villanova sophomore, Bill Heidelberger, outstarted the field sprinting for the first turn. At the same time, a cameraman, focused on the pole vault, backed from the cramped infield onto the track for a better angle. Bill hit the man full speed, pushing him to the outer lane where Jack lowered his shoulder and sent the man and camera over his back and into the disarray of runners, sending some flying over the upper curve and falling onto the Garden floor. Although bruised, no one was seriously hurt. The jittery runners lined up for a new start but ran tentatively, and Jack won the slow heat. He was going to the finals.

The 600 finals were scheduled for Saturday. ABC's Wide World of Sports cut in live for the featured event. Jack held his customary place – the outside lane where he planned to run wide, taking advantage of the gentler curve. The runners set themselves at the line, the gun snapped, and Jack made a beeline for the banked edge forty yards away.

The initial turn is invariably the problem area. Ollan Cassel, the 1964 Olympic 400-meter silver medalist, arrived first, moving from an outside lane toward the center and stepped in front of the Polish Olympian, Andrzej Badenski. Badenski hit the brakes, but his momentum sent him across the turn to the outer lane, where Jack spiked Badenski's ankle, opening a gash that later required stitches. The field of runners bounced over each other and skidded off the track. This time people were hurting.

Someone handed Jack his glasses. He put them on to find a bedlam of bleeding and bruised athletes. The TV people stayed with the dramatic scene for thirty minutes as trainers put people back together. Jack flexed his banged-up right arm and rotated his twisted left ankle. He limped and then sat until the officials called the runners to the line. A trainer approached Jack. "Yerman," he said, "take off your shoe," as he pulled a can of nitrogen spray from his bag. "This will get you through the race." The trainer pointed his can at Jack's puffy ankle and layered on a frosty mist. Jack felt immediate relief.

"How long will it last?" asked Jack.

"Run fast," he replied. "Only until the race is over."

The hum of the audience grew, and Jack set himself in the starting blocks. The runners looked at the man who had been in two pileups in two races. Nerves were on edge, and the track managers called the runners back after two false starts. Then, finally, the gun sounded a third time for a clean start. The field rounded the tight track when Jack tucked behind Badenski with a lap to go. Frank Dolson, a writer for *The Philadelphia Inquirer*, recorded:

```
They all would have been worried men if they
had believed Pinky Sober, the public-address
announcer. "Two laps to go!" he shrieked a
split second before the start of the final lap.
Fortunately, the six runners knew better.
```

Badenski felt Yerman on his neck and knew Jack was where he wanted to be:

> With the fans urging him on, Yerman charged past Badenski in the stretch and regained the championship. As he walked slowly around the banked turn beyond the finish line, catching his breath, little boys ran up and shook his hand. A girl, showing her enthusiasm, jumped up and kissed him. Suddenly, the Garden was alive.
>
> "I don't know how he did it," said John Dunkelberg, who finished a close fourth in the tight race. "He was hurting. I mean, he was really hurting. He's just a great competitor — a helluva competitor!"
>
> Nearby, the press was clamoring for a chance to interview the hero.
>
> "He can't talk to you now," said an official. "He isn't feeling well. He's woozy. He had to go outside for some air."
>
> The explanation made sense — unless you knew Jack Yerman. He was in a phone booth in the lobby of Madison Square Garden, making a long-distance call to Santa Clara, Calif., to tell his wife they were going to Europe.[132]

Jack competed in Europe with the final meet in Berlin. He soon understood the reason for an international meet at the nucleus of the Cold War. The tensions between Communist Russia and the West had festered for years. The two powers had divided Germany into "East" and "West" after World War II. The Allied forces occupied West Berlin, and the Soviets held East Berlin. The Russians wanted all of Berlin, which East Germany surrounded, and in 1948 a Soviet blockade forced the Western powers to employ a large-scale airlift to feed the people in the isolated city. In 1949, the Communists declared Berlin the capital of Communist East Germany.

The East Germans were increasingly dissatisfied with Soviet policies and fled to the West. In 1952, the East German government decreed a prohibited zone three miles deep along the 600-miles it shared with the West. In 1961, the Communists constructed the twenty-six-mile Berlin Wall, cutting off access to the island city. The East and the West's feelings had hit a bitter peak when Jack arrived in 1965, and the West German Parliament proclaimed it would convene in West Berlin rather than Bonn, its capital.

The meet in the heart of Berlin was one of several events to prove to the Communists that life in the West would continue as usual despite efforts to isolate the city. Jack looked towards East Germany's gray skies as the American team left the Holiday Inn, and he watched three Russian MIGS streaking towards them. He saw fire flashing from their wingtips and the fighters dropping shells. Then, when the jets came to the Wall, they pulled to vertical positions, firing their guns straight up while screaming engines rang fear into the walled city. This continued for two frightening hours.

The Western Allies fiercely protested, and the Russians responded with, *What are you going to do about it.* The papers reported Soviet planes conducting military exercises over 300 square kilometers of West German soil and that the ammunition coming from the Russian aircraft were blanks.[133] The performance seemed intent on intimidating those in West Berlin. Nevertheless, the meet would go on.

The track conditions were perfect, the tension in the city created an ideal moment for outstanding performances. Jack ran the race of his life and broke the world record for the indoor 400-meter with a time of 46.9. But gold medalist Mike Larrabee, who Jack had defeated just weeks before, was timed three inches ahead of Jack at 46.8.[(134)]

Margo and Jack returned home through the Black Forest in Germany and visited friends. Jack had run the indoor season better than expected, but he could no longer compete at an international level while pursuing a career and be a father. So Jack hung up his spikes and bid farewell to the oval that had been good to him. It was time to compete in the real world.

CHAPTER 16

Behind Closed Doors

Men in their hungry, selfish greed
Ignore a starving brother's need.
Thy Counsel, Lord.[135]

Coach Brutus Hamilton

Jimmy Hoffa disappeared on July 30, 1975, and would be declared dead a few years later. His remains have never been found. Seven boxes of FBI investigations focused on the mob who had helped him remain in his position as the president of the International Brotherhood of Teamsters from 1957 to 1971, commonly known as the Teamsters Union. He dressed in Italian suits, was a gifted organizer, and had an easy smile and a quick temper. His 5'5 stature and 160 pounds of clean-cut charisma filled the room. He favored friends, isolated threats, and his tenure was marked with corruption and heavy-handed tactics. He had consolidated nearly all the truckers in the United States by 1961, and the Teamsters grew to become a political power behind their master deal maker.

"Good morning, Jack!" Jack liked his boss. Mr. Bardsley had relocated to the Bay Area a decade earlier after designing the Menlo Park offices that he now directed. He was far away from the East's stuffy corporate headquarters and made the South Bay his home. He was active in the local Chamber of Commerce, sat on charity boards, was a member of the local Yacht Club, and respected. He continued, "The contract has lapsed with the Teamsters, and we need to prepare for negotiations."

Jack smiled. He had studied Labor and Industrial Relations at Berkeley, and his brain began to churn. Jack would see how big business and big unions work in real life, and to sit at the table with leaders from the most prominent union in the country would be a great experience.

"The Corporate Vice President of Personnel will be in contact with you." Mr. Bardsley directed, "Get updated on salary and financial information in the meantime. And work with corporate on any information they'll need."

Corporate HR requested that Jack rent a wing of historic St. Francis Hotel on Union Square with its grand lobby, big-band ballrooms, wood-paneled restaurants, and elegant guest rooms. Chandeliers sparkled from the ceiling, and white-marble bathrooms echoed the elegance. So plans proceeded until Jack learned that all limos in the Bay Area had been rented for the 1964 Republican National Convention to be held the same week.

History would show that it was not a coincidence that the Teamsters would be in town at the same time as the Republicans. President John F. Kennedy, a Democrat, was suspicious of the union's leadership. His brother, the Attorney General Robert Kennedy, was on the cusp of convicting Jimmy Hoffa for attempted bribery, fraud, and jury tampering, and Hoffa would be found guilty in a few weeks. Eventually, there would be appeals and another conviction in 1967. Hoffa would go to jail but continue to make the big decisions from prison. President Richard Nixon commuted Hoffa's verdict in 1971, some speculate in exchange for the nearly two-million-member

Teamsters' endorsement.[136] When Jack joined the company's West Coast Division in 1963, history was already in the making as a younger Richard Nixon introduced Barry Goldwater, the Republican nominee for President of the United States, at the Convention in San Francisco.

Jack hired a professional driver and rented a glistening, black, 4-door Cadillac. He waited on the tarmac for the corporate jet and the executive known as the Silver Fox. The plane taxied towards the waiting car. Jack could feel the heat of the exhaust as the high-pitched engines waned and stopped. The fuselage door opened, and an imposing man in a dark suit with a white pocket handkerchief stooped slightly to descend the stairs on a warm July day. The Silver Fox's full head of white hair yielded slightly to the Bay Area's ocean breezes.

Jack greeted the nobility, "Welcome to San Francisco, Sir."

The charismatic executive responded with a New Jersey accent typical of headquarters. "Great to be here, Jack," he said warmly. Jack motioned The Fox to the car. Jack entered on the opposite side and sat next to the man to share documents and provide an update. The executive thumbed through the schedule, nodded at Jack's comments, and asked a few questions. "Good work," he said. "You've got it all in order, and I'll take it from here. You will not be needed for the negotiations."

"Yes, sir," Jack said, hiding his disappointment. Jack looked out the window as the Cadillac crested a San Francisco street. At that moment, he felt small in this big city and awkward next to the Silver Fox. Finally, the driver pulled in front of the hotel and its massive columns. The doorman opened the car while the porter gathered the luggage. The Silver Fox was out and gone in a moment. Jack then directed the driver to return to the office. After that, he found it hard to focus, and a week later, Jack learned that the executive had negotiated a contract giving workers a cost-of-living raise and some benefits.

Jack met regularly with the shop steward, the elected union rep, who is the first contact when an employee has an issue. The shop steward is a mediator between management and the employee. He and Jack worked together to solve problems.

The shop steward confirmed rumors that had trickled back to the office. The union's leaders were invited to stay in the hotel with an open account for unlimited food and liquor, and at the end of a debauchery-filled week, the Fox gave the leaders the contract to sign. Jack had read about "sweetheart agreements" but thought they were a part of labor's dark past.

Three weeks later, Jack's attractive young secretary disclosed that she had spent time with the Fox and was his official *west-coast girlfriend.* A few weeks more and Mr. Bardsley directed Jack to fire the shop steward who had shared the information.

Mr. Bardsley may have noted Jack's trepidation, maybe even some of his discomfort. However, Mr. Bardsley was also a survivor who knew which hills to fight for and when to surrender. He called Jack into his office, "Jack, I think the day you leave here will be a happy one for you." Jack was not fired, nor did he feel pressure to leave, but the chief's remarks permitted him to seek work elsewhere.

Jack found a position with a respected west-coast paper company. Again, Jack connected with the rank and file, and he, again, became friends with the shop steward, who invited him to his home for dinner. Jack and Margo drove into the South Bay's western hills to a small wooden house held together with a patchwork of whitewashed planks. The home was inviting because of its hosts, but its poverty disheartened Jack. As they ate, the shop steward shared that "sweetheart deals" are the norm benefiting management and labor leaders at the expense of rank-and-file employees.

Climbing the corporate ladder, the smart suits, the mixing, mingling, looking out for yourself, and backroom deals were not for Jack. He left the humble home questioning his path and personal mission. He and Margo talked. America's big business would not be for him. He liked the training aspect of his work, and Margo was happy teaching. Maybe teaching would work for him. Margo was pregnant again, she would continue to work, and Jack applied for school.

Coach Brutus Hamilton understood Jack's goodness, intelligence, and tenacity. Hamilton, gifted with a pen and wisdom, wrote:

December 7, 1965

Dear Jack,

I have completed the letters of recommendation. I am in hopes that each of the prospects, the one at San Jose as well as Stanford, will work out to your satisfaction.

It is my very strong feeling that the unpleasant incident at work will eventually be a happy blessing for you. It will lead you into more congenial and servable work and bring you and Margo and the children a more rewarding and fuller life. Most anyone can work for a big company, but you have something special to contribute to the young men and women who will be fortunate enough to come under your guidance. We need inspirational men of high character and lofty principles to teach and guide our children. You and Margo have much to contribute. The next two years may be a little rough, but you'll pull through and come out with flying colors. In the meantime, I'll buy my paper towels and toilet paper from some other source from now on.

So, your little family of three will soon be four. Take good care of yourself and your precious ones. No need for me to tell you to keep your chin up, for I know you'll do that. You and Margo are among the richest people I know. You have a new road of opportunity glistening before you. So, laugh and be jolly and have a good Christmas.

As ever, Coach [137]

Bryce Jordan Yerman was born June 12, 1966, and Jack started the Teacher Education Program at Stanford a week later.

CHAPTER 17

The Blue Wave

I was distressed recently to read a propaganda program put out by the Communists in North Korea concerning the athletic contest they had had for the prisoners of war. It was all the more vicious because it was so well done. I hate to see sports used in a kind of political propaganda, and I hope that our own country can remain civilized enough never to stoop to this.[138]

Coach Brutus Hamilton

Jack enrolled in Stanford's Teacher Education Program for the 1966-67 school year. The Master's program attracted recent graduates and professionals who had decided to change careers. Stanford held intense summer courses that lasted all day and into the night, and in September, Jack received his assignment to teach two sections of U.S. History at Menlo Atherton High School. Atherton had been a railroad stop for wealthy estate owners between San Jose and San Francisco in the mid-1800s. Over the years, the town incorporated, and its estates subdivided while the affluence remained. Today, with a population of nearly 7,000, it ranks among the most expensive zip codes in the United States, with a median home listing price of 7.2 million dollars.[139]

Jack worked with two Stanford buddies, Webster and Ross. The trio designed a game as part of a Stanford teacher-education methods course that would give high-school students a taste of the danger and power of tyranny. *Webster, Ross, and Yerman* researched Korean brainwashing practices, Hitler youth groups, and manifestos from the Communist's Young Pioneers and developed *The Blue Wave Party*, a simulation game with the fear, suspicion, and intrigue of totalitarian states. Game plans[140] included detailed proclamations and support material from some of history's infamous tyrants:

Benito Mussolini

It is the State which, transcending the brief limit of individual lives, represents the central conscience of the nation.

Adolf Hitler

Whatever goal man has reached is due to his originality plus his brutality. Whatever man possesses today in the field of culture is the culture of the Aryan race.

Joseph Stalin

To slacken the tempo would mean falling behind. And those who fall behind, get beaten. No, we refuse to be beaten...That is why Lenin said on the eve of the October Revolution: "Either perish, or overtake and outstrip the advanced capitalist countries."

Mao Tse-Tung

Art and literature are subordinate to politics, but they, in turn, also exert a great influence on politics.

Jack introduced the game's rules on a Friday in preparation for Monday's "day one." The dictator had absolute power without due process. If students "just go along," they earned a B. If students broke the rules, they would be exiled and receive a *D* for that day. Repeat offenders are banished from the game and receive an *F*, symbolizing the fear of banishment to a concentration camp or hard labor in Siberia. Webster, Ross, and Yerman were the totalitarians who maintained their control in this game.

Jack saluted the class and proclaimed, "Strength through discipline!"

Students thrust fists in the air and responded in unison, "Strength through discipline!"

Jerry stood, "It's not fair to get an *F* for playing a game!" and he stomped out of the room. The game-players observed the Party symbols — students wore blue tape over their hearts, carried I.D. cards, greeted comrades, saluted dictators, and recited the creed:

Strength through discipline!
Strength through involvement!
Disciplined involvement empowers group victory!
Total group victory is individual victory!

Party members could not mingle in groups of three or more without a dictator's permission, and the teachers dealt harshly with a student who broke the rules. In class, the dictator announced offenses, and a bodyguard escorted the condemned out of the room as classmates chanted in unison, ENEMY OF THE PARTY, ENEMY OF THE PARTY.

The Stanford trio had taken rules from a 1943 Soviet Ministry of Education directive prohibiting slouching and touching elbows on the desk, and for this game enemies of the Party were punished with worksheets and textbook assignments. Harsh measures preserved the Party, and it was about this time in Jack's explanation that Jerry left the room.

A student could win the game if they wrote a plan to overthrow the dictator, organized a revolution, and replaced the teacher with a democracy. The revolutionaries had to find five Party members willing to sign the plan, keep it a secret, and place it in a designated spot without detection. Webster, Ross, and Yerman would call students at night, offering extra credit for reports of developing plans and conspiring students. The tyrants neutralized the opposition with the "Secret Police," which compelled players to follow the Party line.

Jack awoke the second day at his usual hour to drive the forty-mile commute from Santa Clara to Palo Alto. He turned the key on his VW Bug. It whimpered. He opened the rear engine cover to find a stick of toy dynamite and a note saying *BOMB. You're dead!* Jack put the car back together and drove to work to find Webster ambushed in his classroom and tied to his chair. Ross showed up at his classroom door, wet. Several masked students wearing hoods had jumped from behind a curtain in the lobby and soaked him with water-filled machine guns. The teachers called an emergency assembly. "Killing a dictator will not eliminate a totalitarian government," the trio explained. "A new dictator will simply take over. You need to find a better way to form a democracy."

Jack looked out the window to see Jerry sitting on the grass, glaring back at him. On Wednesday, Jerry walked into the room and challenged, "If everyone leaves with me, there will be no dictator, and Mr. Yerman loses!" The students jumped from their seats and headed for the door.

Jack retorted, "If any of you go out that door, you will receive an *F.*" Menlo Atherton Students loved grades, and all returned and sat down.

Each day, Jack arrived late to class – a scowl across his brow and holding up a crumpled paper with illegible notes. "Confess, and be forgiven," he cried out, "If you stand and confess sins against the Party you will be forgiven, but if I read the Police Report and you are in it, you will be punished!" Several students stood and confessed transgressions that the dictator knew nothing about. Even more alarming, students began denouncing their friends.

Game players had entered the brainwashing phase used by Nazi youth groups and Korean prisoner-of-war camps. Wardens used rewards and punishments to condition the POWs to write confessions and expose others. Exposing fellow prisoners was essential to a self-policing state. The Chinese reduced guards to a minimum as prisoners became group citizens. The Americans monitored themselves to the point of revealing escape plots so the whole group would stay out of trouble. Some soldiers became turncoats at the end of the war and chose to live in Communist China.[141]

Hitler had called for mass rallies where he commenced at a slow tempo and increased pace and volume to a crescendo where he shouted passionately with the crowd cheering. The Stanford trio did the same at their assemblies — the tenor in the dictators' voices rang forceful as students shouted *Strength through discipline! Strength through discipline!* The students felt special and better than others in the school, and the movement isolated potential leaders like Jerry.

The game took off at Menlo Atherton, and soon other students recruited themselves into the experiment. Webster, Ross, and Yerman worried when players showed up at school in army fatigues and combat boots. It seemed the game filled a need for belonging, and some avoided school altogether to escape the game. Amy was upset because her friends believed she was with the Secret Police and stopped talking to her. "Please tell everyone that I'm not, Mr. Yerman, I'm not…," she pleaded. Finally, Jack presented the problem to the group, and as a true tyrant, he informed the class that Amy *was* a member of the Secret Police. She put her head down on her desk and cried. The Police had power. To maintain control, the teachers purged the Police, switching them often, following Hitler, Stalin, and Mao's practice of removing officials to preserve power.

Students reported that nearby Palo Alto High School had started a branch of The Wave, and Menlo Atherton's administration asked Webster,

Ross, and Yerman how this game would end. The trio had planned to grad-
ually conclude the game over six sections of classes throughout the day.
Webster taught first and second, Ross had periods three and four, and after
lunch, Jack taught periods five and six. Webster's game ended when he was
jumped by a gang of students who tied him up and stuffed him under his
desk. Ross and Yerman ran down to the classroom on a tip to find Webster's
triumphant students eating popcorn and watching "Our Gang" films.

Ross closed his part of the game without incident, and now it was Jack's
turn. He had planned to finish the game with a survey and discuss what students had learned about freedoms they had been denied. But, instead, the
department chair came to the door, "Mr. Yerman. There has been some trouble, and you're needed at the vice-principal's office. I can stay with the class."

Jack headed out the door and down the corridor for Mr. Glover's office,
a demanding, bald, towering, *no-neck* vice-principal and former football
guard with a thick scar across his cheek and a broken tooth. Jack noticed
a black Cadillac limousine parked as Jack approached the administration
building. He entered Mr. Glover's office, who sat behind his desk – his arms
crossed. Jerry's parents sat across from him. Jack thought, "Jerry's father had
taken time off from running a Fortune 500 company to straighten out this
green teacher. "

Mr. Glover addressed Jack in his deep voice, "These people have something to say to you."

Jerry's father rose to his full six-foot-seven-inch stature. Jack gulped. The
executive extended his hand to the teacher, smiled, and said, *"Thank you!"*

Jack was confused.

"Thank you for the greatest learning experience my son has ever had."

Mr. Glover laughed, "Jack, you have lost the game, and you don't even
know it!"

Jerry's parents, Mr. Glover, and Jack walked back to the classroom to find Jerry in charge, sitting on a desk in front of the class eating a cookie. Jerry's father had sent the food, and with mouths full, the class smiled triumphantly. Jerry raised his soda to Jack and grinned. Fear had removed Jack from the classroom, and Jerry had replaced it with a democracy. The unity and will of the citizens had left the dictator powerless.

Jack later played the game at Chico High School. He waited a few years between experiments to prevent brothers and sisters from sharing their information with a new generation. Each time he played the game, students immersed themselves into the slogans, the colors, saluting, and conforming. Jack's coworkers were amazed at how quickly students fell under the dictator's control, and it seemed to Jack that each new generation betrayed each other far more.

Jack received requests from former students asking for copies of The Blue Wave to use in their classrooms:

```
Date: Thu, 27 May 1999
From: Kiri & Michael
Subject: Blue Wave

Mr. Yerman—thanks for sending me a copy of The
Blue Wave Party. I'm forwarding it to a friend
who's a secondary teacher in London. Given 1) the
ethnic mix at his school and 2) the recent racist
"nail-bombings" in London, it could be timely.

I am looking at The Wave in the context of what
happened in Cambodia under the Khmer Rouge and the
period of Vietnamese liberation/occupation fol-
lowing 1979. History is something that Cambodia
cannot escape from. Yet, due to agreements signed
in the early '90s on reconciliation, there is no
```

mechanism for educating children about the Khmer Rouge period in schools now.

One of my favorite stories is from a Khmer friend who was watching television with her family — when the grandmother pointed at the images of forced labour on the screen and said that this was life during the "Pol Pot time," her grandson openly scoffed and said that was impossible, Cambodia was never like that.

And, to think it's only been 20 years.[142]

A fictional novel entitled *The Wave* was published in 1981 and became required reading for students worldwide. An ABC prime-time drama followed. The book and TV production were based on a "classroom experiment that went too far," declared the book's cover. A history teacher at Palo Alto had played the game in 1969. He called his version *The Third Wave* and said, "It was one of the most frightening events I have ever experienced in the classroom."[143]

Jack attempted to contact the teacher over the years. He wanted to share stories and compare notes but was unable to connect until Jack's son, Blake, found the teacher's email and reached out in 2013:

From: blakeyerman
Sent: Thursday, August 8, 2013, 8:49 AM
Subject: "The Blue Wave"

You may be interested in getting the original lesson plans. The original experiment was done at a high school in Menlo Atherton. The entire story is even better than the novel. There is a teacher that remembers the original teachers involved.

I am not writing this to detract from the fantas-
tic success of the novel and movie. There is no
ulterior motive other than completing an already
good story. I am sure that you would enjoy spending time with him.[144]

The teacher replied a few hours later, "I doubt very much this person wants to meet 'what really happened!'"[145]

CHAPTER 18

Bulls and Bears

Formal education often tames and dilutes a man, robs him of his freshness, originality, and in some cases, I've seen it almost destroy the most likable traits in one's personality.[146]

Coach Brutus Hamilton

Jack assigned students a typical economics project of tracking stocks on the New York Stock Exchange. Students would buy, sell, and see gains or losses. Jack hoped this would help students understand the 1929 stock-market crash. Each student received 10,000 Yerm-Dollars to invest.

1967 proved to be a bull market.[147] Students boasted, "I made five-hundred dollars on Xerox," or, "I made six hundred on IBM." All were enthusiastic until a student protested, "Mr. Yerman, those boys really invested ten-thousand dollars!"

"What do you mean?" asked Jack.

"They put ten thousand *real dollars* into the market," complained the student.

A group of boys confirmed they had invested real money.

"You're kidding!" Jack exclaimed.

"Don't worry, Mr. Yerman, we invest all the time."

Jack began to understand his class better. One student's father was a vice president at CBS, and another was the president of Ampex Corporation — the people who would revolutionize home videos when they invent the recording heads for the VCR — and another had a grandfather who invented color film. Many homes around the schools were luxurious mansions by any standards.

"That's not fair, Mr. Yerman," said some students. "They are making lots of money. We want to *invest* in the market and make *real money* like those guys."

"We can do that," a student added. "We can set up an investment club."

"What's that?" asked Jack.

The student explained that each class member would contribute to making a joint investment. "Let's do it!" a student chimed in, and another suggested, "We can each put in $5.00."

It seemed like a great idea to Jack, and the sum wasn't so large that anyone would suffer a significant loss. The class agreed, and soon the *Mr. Yerman Investment Club* had a total of $150.

"What stock should we buy?" The club selected four students to study options. The class heard reports about IBM and Linton Industries selling for 20 to 30 dollars a share. Everything seemed expensive, and the club rejected all proposals. After several weeks, the class still sat on its $150.

A few days later, Jack entered the faculty room to find a note in his mailbox:

The Stock Committee is holding a meeting today, at lunch, in the library.

The group heard from Ronald. "Last night, my dad returned from traveling to Africa. He's the vice president of Bechtel Industries in charge of operations in that continent." Bechtel was a large international development firm based in San Francisco. This company constructed Hoover Dam and installed pillars for the Oakland Bay Bridge deep in the Bay's floor. They built cities, bridges, and road systems worldwide and eventually would make the tubes under San Francisco for its commuter trains. Ron continued, "My dad told my mom that Zambia discovered the largest deposit of pure copper, and its stock will go on sale next week."

In the heart of Africa, Northern Rhodesia had declared its independence from Great Britain to become the Republic of Zambia in 1964, while most neighboring countries continued as British colonies under white minority rule. Meanwhile, neighboring Rhodesia had been hit with United Nations sanctions for human rights violation, and it retaliated by impeding Zambia's railroad shipments at its border.[148] The Copper Corridor ran from Zambia, through Rhodesia, and on to the port of Beira in Mozambique, where copper was loaded on freighters and shipped north through to the Red Sea, the Suez Canal, and across the Mediterranean for copper hungry European markets. Zambia consistently opposed Rhodesia's white supremacist government, yet the countries' economies relied on each other, and the critical railroad route opened again to trade.[149] The papers reported:

> **London, May 31 [1966]** — A Rhodesian Railways train, carrying a consignment of Zambian copper and zinc, crossed the Victoria Falls Bridge into Rhodesia today without hindrance...News of the Zambian copper shipment across the Rhodesian border came after the London Stock Market closed, but copper shares [moved] higher just before the official close.[150]

The committee agreed to purchase Zambian Copper. They learned the stock would be sold "over the counter," meaning the sale could not meet the requirements of a large exchange. The committee would contact a broker and buy the stock directly from the company. At first, the broker could not find information about Zambian Copper, but after some confusing minutes, he answered, "Oh, yes, here it is. Zambia. It's new and sells for seventy-five cents a share." The club purchased two hundred shares of stock which was much more exciting than five shares of IBM.

Each day, students asked, "How's our stock doing?" "Nothing. It's still at seventy-five cents a share."

Two weeks later, the San Francisco Chronicle business section featured Zambia's large copper deposits and the world's hunger for copper. The stock rose that day to $2.50. The club was now worth $500. By the end of the week, the stock was at $5.00, and the club was worth $1,000. The class wanted to know more about Zambia! A student reported:

> *Zambia is a new, third-world country, landlocked in the center of Africa and developing its natural resources. Zambia and Rhodesia are neighbors with a railway bridge near Victoria Falls. Rhodesian trains carry needed coal to Zambia and Zambia uses the Railroad to export its copper to the coast and on to Europe.*[151] *The value of Zambia's copper projection soared to an all-time high last year.*[152] *Zambian copper has jumped 66% in the world markets.*[153] *Zambia's first Lady prefers the modest national wrap-around dress to the modern miniskirts, and she hopes to see copper, the country's biggest export, used in kitchens around the world.*[154]

The class decided to keep the stock for a while. The stock remained stable for several weeks and then started to move again. With the war in Vietnam and trouble in the Middle East, the demand for copper rose sharply, and Zambian Copper jumped to $15.00 a share. The class now had $3,000!

Students talked stocks every day, and Jack spent a little class time on the topic, and, at this point, he began to have trouble with the school. The counseling department was asking, "Why does everyone want to transfer to Yerman's class?"

"It is probably because we have money," he said.

Students began to ask, "How are we going to spend the money?"

Jack suggested. "Sell now and divide the earnings. Or at least sell some of the stock and return the initial investments."

The class clamored, "No, let's keep the stock and sell at the end of the year!"

Things in Zambian Copper got crazier. President Johnson escalated Operation Rolling Thunder, destroying the North Vietnam economy and demoralizing its people.[155] As a result, Zambian stocks jumped to $30.00. Jack suggested they sell and buy something the school could use — maybe a lovely drinking fountain. The class offered, No, *let's have the mother-of-all-parties!* The class formed a sub-committee to talk about chartering a bus and reserving a nightclub with a live band.

I am in trouble, Jack thought. He needed help. The principal sat behind his desk, listening to the greenhorn teacher. "No problem," he said, "I'll take care of it." The principal explained to the class that the Board must approve all field trips outside of the school district, and this trip would not be approved."

"Whew," sighed Jack.

When the principal left, one of the students declared, "My dad's a corporate lawyer. So he'll know what to do." And the next day, the class *announced that* the party would take place the day after school let out.

The stock increased to $40.00 a share, and the class started talking about an overnight trip. It was difficult to teach history. Jack figured that he could avoid the party if he could get the students to sell the stock and divide the money. "No, Mr. Yerman, we are hanging on and selling the last week of school."

Zambian Copper plateaued, and as the end of the school year approached, students focused on finals. Jack put the stock project out of his mind for a brief period until Tuesday of the last week of school. He found Ron leaning on the classroom door. "Ronald, what's up?" Jack asked.

"Haven't you heard? About the war?"

"Sure, the Vietnam War is on the news every day."

"No, not that war, the other war." Ronald was talking about the latest conflict between Egypt and Israel. Arab mobs burned the U.S. and British Consulates, reporters had been caught in the crossfire, and Egyptian trucks sat burning in nearby Gaza.[156] The Egyptian president had closed the Suez Canal while Israeli Phantom Jets headed across the Mediterranean, destroying everything that looked like Egyptian military. [157]

The stock plummeted to 50 cents a share. With the canal paralyzed and no way to ship Zambian copper, the students' high hopes for the mother-of-all-parties sank with the falling share prices. Jack sighed a deep breath of relief. He'd get his teaching credential after all.

CHAPTER 19

Recall

People break Thy moral laws
And sins, not virtues, gain applause
They Guidance, Lord [158]

Coach Brutus Hamilton

The Junior senator, Joseph McCarthy, stood before the Ohio County Women's Republican Club in Wheeling, West Virginia, at an event meant to honor Abraham Lincoln's birthday. He raised a piece of paper with handwritten notes and waved it before his audience. "I have here in my hand a list of 205 [State Department employees] that were known to the Secretary of State as being members of the Communist Party and who nevertheless are still working…" [159]

McCarthy attacked without evidence, and over the next few weeks, his number varied wildly from 205 to 57, to 10, to 81. His claims that The Reds had infiltrated America grew to include Hollywood and America's schools. Venomous misinformation infected the country in the 1950s, and its contagion lingers in Deep State conspiracies today.

Joseph McCarthy served as a World War II intelligence officer for the US Marines. To ease the monotony in Guadalcanal, McCarthy belted himself into the tail gunner's seat of a bomber, went aloft, and blasted at coconut trees. The Henderson Field, Public Relations Officer, crafted a press release proclaiming McCarthy's had fired more shots than any marine in history, and his buddies gave him an award for destroying the island's plant life. A few weeks later, McCarthy returned to the Public Relations Hut waving a stack of clippings. "This is worth 50,000 votes to me," he said with a smile. The two men toasted a cup to celebrate the making of Tail-Gunner Joe. [160]

McCarthy continued inventing stories and plagiarized a letter from Admiral Chester Nimitz, the commander in chief of the U.S. Pacific Fleet:

> Although suffering from a severe leg injury, [Captain McCarthy] refused to be hospitalized and continued to carry out his duties as an intelligence officer in a highly efficient manner. His courageous devotion to duty was in keeping with the highest traditions of the naval service. [161]

An ambitious McCarthy returned to Wisconsin, and riding a wave of America's admiration of its heroes, Tail Gunner Joe ran for the U.S. Senate and won. The bullish freshman rejected the Senate's historical traditions, and McCarthy soon earned a reputation for being difficult. His political career faltered, so he fostered rumors that communists had infiltrated America's institutions and he would become its liberator. The Senate tolerated McCarthy, and some rode the wave of his conspiracy theories, but his lies eventually caught up to him. The Senate censured him, his health declined, and the forty-seven-year-old senator, addicted to alcohol and morphine, died in 1958. The practice of reckless accusations and inflammatory attacks on progressive adversaries remains associated with his name to this day. [162]

In 1963, Life Magazine reported on the turmoil in the small Northern California town of Paradise. McCarthy's followers decided that the high school had been infiltrated by antireligious Communists and resolved to purge socialism from Paradise's public schools. The attackers devised a plan to conceal a tape recorder in a book:

```
[Virginia Franklin's] social studies classes,
filled with debate, are encouraged to read mate-
rial of widely divergent points of view, from the
liberal to the extremes of the right wing. This
year Mrs. Franklin won an award from the respected
Freedoms Foundation as an outstanding teacher of
"the American credo."
    But her pedagogy has also won the enmity of
the American Legion post in Paradise, some John
Birch Society members and other townspeople. They
accuse Mrs. Franklin of subverting the patriotism
of the youth with leftist ideas [and]of being a
Communist....
    Last week the furor came to a climax with an
election to choose three new school board members.
To oust not only Mrs. Franklin but the school prin-
cipal and superintendent....
    [The] bait was a prayer. The class is about to
begin a mock U.S. Senate hearing, and an 18-year-
old named Ty Blount, seeking evidence that the
teacher is antireligious, rises to propose an open-
ing prayer hoping she might object. At this point
Mrs. Franklin is unaware that a tiny recorder,
concealed in the hollowed-out textbook under Ty's
desk, is taking down everything.
    But the mock committee vetoes the prayer while
Mrs. Franklin remains silent. As the class ends,
Mrs. Franklin, now tipped off by the principal,
```

abruptly flips open the book as Ty Blount tries to
fend her off, yelping, "Oh, no you don't! That's my
book!"....

Shaken by the exposure..., Ty then asked the
principal to drive him to the real estate office
of his father, Walter Blount,...[where] the elder
Blount, who had helped Ty devise the trap, dismissed the incident. "We've got a vault full of
tapes," the father said. "Ty carries [the machine]
almost every day." [163]

The Paradise Unified School District sided with the teacher, so the
McCarthyites harassed the Board's businesses. A moderate Board member's
son, now grown, shared his family's pain with Jack years later:

*By the time it all shook out in 1966, my parents' marriage was on
the rocks. The family's moving and storage business suffered from
costly vandalism, leading to my parents' divorce. They had been
business in Paradise since 1942. The situation broke my father's
heart. He drank more, became an alcoholic, but eventually beat
that. My mother was equally hurt, but she's the one that initiated
the divorce because she needed to move on. They remained friends
until he died.[*]*

Jack had accepted a job as a history teacher and coach at Chico High
School, and Margo would teach English at nearby Pleasant Valley High
School. They fell in love with the Town of Paradise nestled in the Sierra
Nevada foothills about 25 minutes up the hill from Chico. Jack and Margo
loaded their new 1967 VW van with the family's possessions and left the Bay
Area for their new home.

---

* *2016 Author Interview.*

Margo Teaching at P.V. in Chico
(Jack and Margo Yerman Collection)

By the time the Yermans arrived in the summer of '67, an ultra-con-
servative slate controlled the school board and took on the duties of hiring
teachers and running the academic program. In September, Bruce would
attend Kindergarten, so Jack and Margo drove twenty miles from Paradise
to the small logging town of Sterling City to participate in a board meeting.
Jack and Margo entered the school's cafeteria and sat in chairs along the
center aisle. Jack had a beard, wore a long-sleeve plaid shirt, and looked
like a local logger.

Trustee Barrette spoke. "Our schools have drifted from a moral
compass." He turned and looked at the Paradise High School English
Chair sitting in the front row. "Teachers are filling young minds with filth
from books promoting sex, suicide, and murder." The teacher sat tall; his
hands turned white as he gripped his notebook. Mr. Barrette continued,

"Therefore, all books not approved by the Board's Curriculum Committee are prohibited."

Margo fidgeted in her chair and whispered to Jack. He raised his hand to speak, "My name is Jack. You are doing amazing things for our children, but the worst of it is still in the curriculum. It has rape, incest, prostitution, and murder!" Mr. Barrette leaned forward, believing this man to be his ally. "If you're going to protect our children," Jack continued, "don't forget about Shakespeare!"

Jack sat down, and Margo squeezed his hand.

Mr. Barrett shook his head, "That's classic literature and does not fall into this category."

The following week, and over the principal's objections, the superintendent removed two high-school teachers from the social studies department who had circulated a grievance letter. When the teachers' union asked the superintendent why he pulled the pair, he retorted, "If you don't know, I won't tell you." And by the fall of 1968, whisper campaigns accused the school principal of harassing girls.[*]

Jack and Margo welcomed the Christmas break to visit Margo's parents and give thought to living in the town that had persecuted Virginia Franklin. The van hummed south on Highway 99, Jack behind the wheel and Margo sitting next to him. Bruce and Bryce slept on bench seats in the back.

"Each board meeting is bigger, and people are angrier," observed Jack.

---

[*] *The 1968 teachers' union president shared, "I think that many of their tactical behaviors were taught by an ultraconservative organization, saying, 'This is how you get in and this is how you get rid of people.'"*

"And I don't want to be pessimistic," Margo continued, "but I don't think we can buy a home in Paradise." She thought for a moment watching the rhythmic rows of sleeping peach trees drifting by under the backdrop of a grey California winter day. Then, her mental gears turned, and her voice picked up its tempo, "But I'm not ready to give up. We need a meeting!" she exclaimed.

Margo called Bev Corry after the holiday. Her husband, Mel, was a down-to-earth family physician, and they had children in the schools. Bev knew people, called her friends, and Margo set the agenda. The group met at the Corry home and agreed to support moderate candidates in April's election, write letters to the paper, and canvass the community.

The people of Paradise woke up, and March's school board was moved to the high-school gym. Every seat on the floor was taken, the back bleachers full, and people stood against the walls. The Board had placed a discussion item on the agenda to terminate three teachers and demote the High School and Middle School principals to the classroom. The trustees sat on the stage overlooking the crowd. Margo addressed the Board. "There are many who would like to speak but can't, so I'll ask a question." Then, Margo turned to the crowd, "I invite everyone who wishes to keep the three high-school teachers in question to please stand." A "whoosh" went through the auditorium as nearly all rose to their feet. "Thank you," she said. "And I'd like a standing vote of those who wish to retain the principals." Another "whoosh" of supporters stood.

Margo turned to the Board, "If you do not return the teachers and retain the principals, you no longer represent the majority in this community; you have disclaimed your responsibility to the electorate of this community and the children and grandchildren of Paradise!" The crowd applauded.

The Board dismissed themselves for an executive session and returned two hours later with a decree: the principals would be demoted and assigned to the classroom; the social studies teachers issued reprimands. "This meeting is adjourned," belted the president to the astonished crowd. The closing blow of the gavel reverberated across the hall.

The committee meeting at the Corry home had grown to more than 50 members. Margo convened the group that same night, with the addition of all four principals, including the two just demoted and teachers, doctors, businessmen and women, and parents young and old. The group drafted its plan, *Recall: Our Only Recourse*. The campaign raised $4,000 in less than a week and would collect 3,700 of the 1,800 required signatures for a special election.

The County Clerk set the Recall Election for Tuesday, June 24, 1969. Margo drafted news releases and organized volunteers who donated time and money, solicited funds, invited friends to coffee klatches, and campaigned door to door. When the opposition boycotted businesses, the Recall friends supported those establishments. Tom, the teachers-union rep, remembered, "We left no stone unturned."

Throughout the campaign, Jack and Margo maintained their teaching jobs in Chico, and Jack coached the High School track team, and he asked the art department to sketch the school's mascot on the side of his VW van before taking a group of runners to a Bay Area meet. Students painted a menacing black panther on the van's sides with outstretched claws and foreboding red eyes. Jack liked the mascot and kept it on the car after the meet. At the same time, the Black Panther Party in Oakland promoted militant force for protection and to achieve the civil rights of blacks. In a few weeks, FBI Director J. Edgar Hoover would proclaim, "The Black Panther party, without question, represents the greatest threat to the internal security of the country."[164]

The Feather River Times took photos of Jack's van and claimed that a white, balding, bespectacled history teacher was a leader in the Black Panthers. A grey-haired grandmother confronted Jack at the grocery store parking lot, wagging her finger at him. "We have photos of you and your Black Panther meetings," she warned," and we're watching you!" The paper also printed a photo of Margo on the front page, and next to it, the headline, "Recall Chairman Denies Misuse of Funds." The layout suggested fraudulent activity, but it wasn't until the reader turned the page that the article was about an election in a distant city. The Feather River Times refused to retract the article about Margo, so Jack took the case to Reginald Watt, an attorney in Chico and a former judge, and he discovered a far-right group from out of the area funding the paper. So Jack and Margo sued the paper for slander.

A week before the elections, committee members received hate mail – poorly written letters that had been pounded out on an old typewriter. The letters warned committee members to back off and claimed that candidate Lucy Flood, a longtime churchgoer, was a secret atheist. The messages were signed, *Americans Against Communism and Crime.*

Dozens of recall workers gathered at the headquarters on the day of the election to sip on Paradise apple cider and nibble on homemade cookies. The results trickled in, hope grew, and the atmosphere turned festive. The recall had two YES votes for every NO. "We did it!" celebrated Margo with a double fist pump in the air.

The new School Board passed a "no confidence" vote, and the superintendent resigned. The liable suite against the *Feather River Times* would take two more years[165] and the court eventually awarded Jack and Margo its assets. On a stormy night before the handoff, the defendants scattered files, furniture, and print machines on the rain-soaked street, destroying the paper for good.

CITIZENS FOR RECALL
THANKS

the hundreds of Paradise citizens for their personal involvement and sacrifice of time and dollars. Your efforts to return stability and dignity to our schools are proof of your concern for Paradise children.

Citizens Committee for Recall
Margo Yerman, Chairman

(Jack and Margo Yerman Collection)

CHAPTER 20

The Podium

Thy colored peoples stand in awe
Of cruel, bitter racial law
Thy Mercy, Lord [166]

Coach Brutus Hamilton

Mr. Yerman, is Martin Luther King a Communist?"

Jack looked across the classroom at Stacy. "Why do you ask?" he responded.

Jamie, a black student, interrupted, "Because a teacher is showing a film that says Dr. King is a Communist and the FBI is on to him!"

The Civil Rights movement was front and center for civic-minded high-school students in 1969. It had been just nine years since four black students sat at a Woolworth's whites-only lunch counter in North Carolina. And three years later, Alabama's Governor George Wallace avowed, "segregation now, segregation tomorrow, and segregation forever!" That same year, he stood at the doors at the University of Alabama, blocking the entrance of two black students. Soon, a quarter of a million people would march on Washington and hear Martin Luther King ring out, "I have a dream…" And a KKK bomb killed four young black girls at a Church in Birmingham.

The 1964 Civil Rights Act was signed, and a year later, demonstrators protested voter suppression by marching from Selma to Birmingham on what became Bloody Sunday. Meanwhile, the John Birch Society proclaimed, "*Civil Rights is a perfect example of Communist tactics.*" [167]

Dr. King was killed in 1968. George Wallace campaigned for president of the United States, shouting *Stand up for America while denouncing political parties, civil rights, and the free press.*[168] Meanwhile, conspiracists back home spread rumors that the radical Black Panthers from Oakland were planning to burn the Town of Paradise to the ground, and some fearful citizens on the ridge believed a secret Chinese army trained in the woods above Sterling City.*

Black athletes at the 1968 Mexico City Olympics recognized they had a world stage. An international TV audience watched Tommie Smith and John Carlos win the Gold and Bronze medals in the 200-meter sprint. The champions stood on the victory podium without shoes to symbolize poverty. Smith added a scarf for unity while Carlos wore a neckless to represent lynching.[169] Smith bowed his head in prayer during the anthem, and both athletes raised gloved fists. Australian Silver-medalist, Peter Norman, added the *Olympic Project for Human Rights* pin to his uniform in solidarity.†

Tommie Smith said at the press conference, "If I win, I am an American, not a black American. But if I did something bad, then they would say 'a Negro'. We are black, and we are proud of being black. Black America will understand what we did tonight." [170]

---

*   *Jack remembers the fear of some Paradise residents who shared the rumor.*

†   Smith and Carlos on Podium:
   ▶ https://bit.ly/1968Fist

The United States Olympic Committee suspended Smith and Carlos from the Olympic Village.[*] The pair returned home to condemnation, unemployment, and death threats. The Australian, Norman, who had opportunities to condemn Carlos and Smith, never did.[171] He, too, struggled to find work in Australia.[172][†]

California High School teachers enjoyed academic freedom in the 1960s and 70s,[173] and the Northern California Coordinator for the John Birch Society and a former teacher, was a regular visitor at Chico High School.[174] He explained that Joseph McCarthy's 1953 Internal Senate Subcommittee had exposed Communist subversion in the government and that the Communists were behind the Vietnam peace marches. He alleged that the press would not report the real story[175] and called Civil Rights leaders Cesar Chavez and Dr. King agitators and asserted: "the Communists are working hard to infiltrate the American Negro Population." He brought films to substantiate the claims.[176]

Jack rose from his desk and asked his students, "What do you think?"

Allan, a white kid who enjoyed attention more than details, woke up and grinned, "Yeah, he's a Commie!"

"Shut up," said Jamie, turning to glare at Allan.

Natasha fidgeted in her seat. "Mr. Yerman," she implored, "this is the BS we get when we come to school. What can we do?"

Jack contemplated for a moment, "Let's invite Tommie Smith to the school." The students sat silent – maybe a bit stunned. *Tommie Smith...?*

"Yes!" Natasha grinned. "Let's do it."

---

*   ABC Sports Commentator Howard Cosell on Smith and Carlos
    [▷] http://bit.ly/Cosell68

†   *In 1970, Jack chaired the first Chico High School committee to establish graduation requirements.*

Jack in the Classroom at Chico High School

Yerman and Smith had run together at a Santa Clara track club. Smith competed in the indoor 60-yard sprint, and Jack raced the 660, and they shared the baton in the mile relay.[177] Both had been big-name attractions to the indoor circuit. Sportswriters plugged Smith as a World Record holder[178] and Jack for his track-smarts.[179] Jack telephoned his teammate and invited him to speak with students. Tommie agreed.[180] Jack remembers this was Tommie's first public event following the Olympics.

Smith asked Jack to set up a meeting with a few black students before speaking to the student body. Bill, Charles, Clay, and Scotty[181] waited in front of the school. The boy's giddy enthusiasm hung in the laughter that condensed on the brisk pre-dawn air. Jack's van pulled up to the curb, collected the boys, and motored down Cohasset Road to Chico's Regional Airport to meet their guest.

Jack had made reservations for breakfast at Sambo's in downtown Chico.* The pair of gold medalists with the four boys entered the restaurant to a hum of conversation mixing with the morning aroma of hot coffee. Social clubs, bible study groups, and business people regularly gathered at Sambos Restaurant, and on this day, farmers and ranchers enjoyed the winter reprieve on a day forecasting rain. Customers looked from their newspapers as the 6'3" Smith and the four black boys walked to their table. Jack sensed the whispers from those who had read a letter in the morning's Enterprise-Record:

> Dear Editor,
>
> You will all remember San Jose State sprinter Tommie Smith? You will also remember he won a gold medal? We Americans were very proud. Then, during the presentation of these medals, our pride was shattered. In the eyes of the world, this young man dishonored the flag of his country with his "black power" salute.
>
> I understand this man will be a guest speaker at Chico High school on Feb. 5 (today).
>
> There are many sports figures available for this type of function, who are not only excellent speakers but loyal Americans. Why subject our young people to this kind of influence? Of all the good in the country, why reach for the bad? I strongly protest.[182]

The boys sat awestricken with Mr. Smith, the 200-meter world record holder and the son of farm laborers. Tommie left behind a life of harvesting cotton when he enrolled at San Jose State. Tommie had noticed that black

---

* *At the corner of 9th Ave. and The Esplanade in Chico, CA, where a Starbucks is now located.*

athletes were routinely pushed out of sciences and humanities and directed to physical education courses. While the practice brought accolades to sports programs, professional employment for the black athlete following school was unlikely.[183] Tommie majored in social science and was in his last semester to be a teacher. He advocated for equality in housing, integrating social clubs, and employing black students at the university. Beyond campus, Smith helped create the *Olympic Project for Human Rights,* a civil-rights group that boycotted the New York Athletic Club that barred Puerto Rican, Black, and Jewish members. The group lobbied to restore Mohamed Alli's World Heavyweight Boxing Title, and it opposed apartheid countries participating in the Olympics.[184]

Tommie looked to the young men after ordering breakfast. Jack remembers Smith giving instructions to the boys for the day: "I'm asking each of you to share at the assembly what it's like to be black at school."

The boys fidgeted but could not ignore the Olympian's resolve. "We can do that," they answered.

The school scheduled the speech during an Activities Period. Students could choose to read in the library, paint in the art room, or play in the gymnasium, but nearly all sat on the polished floor of the cafeteria to hear Mr. Smith. Never had this many attended a voluntary assembly.[185] A student stopped Jack as he made his way through the overflow crowd, "Mr. Yerman, you're not going to let him say bad things about white people, are you?"

"We're all going to learn something today," Jack smiled.

ASB President Jeff Carter stepped up to the small, makeshift stage and pulled the microphone closer. "We are pleased to welcome the 200-meter world-record holder and Olympic gold medalist Tommie Smith to Chico High School and glad he would take his time to talk with us about race and civil rights." The students clapped.

Tommie took his place at the podium and thanked the students for the invitation. Before I speak," he said as he motioned to the boys sitting behind him, "my friends on the stage have some things to share with you today."

The students sat quietly on the floor as the first of their friends took the stage. Bill Berry adjusted the microphone from Tommie's height and took a moment to look at his peers. He had shared friendly banter at school, but on this topic, he was candid:

> *The race problem is pretty bad right now. It's hard to get along with your fellow man, but it is something we should learn to do. I don't think another civil war is right, so I guess we just better sit down and have a long discussion about what's happening.* [186] *The black man is tired of being a boy.* [187]

Two more of the boys spoke, and then Alios Scott Jr., a cheerful soul and the starting halfback on the football team and a baseball player took his turn at the podium. "Scotty," as the students called him, looked across the room:

> *I am friends with many of you. You all know and seem to like Scotty but many of you have never understood the tough times for the minority students. No invite to your homes after school or "Hey, party with us" after the game. That's what it's like to be at Chico High School. When the school day's over – it's over. Yes, I have good friends, but what I said still holds. Not much happens past the school day for minority students.* [188]

When Scotty returned to his seat, Tommie stood and thanked the young men. He looked at the overflow crowd and thanked the students for choosing to listen and discuss what it is like to be black in America. He shared growing up poor, a farm laborer, and making it through high school and into college. Tommie, who was ten units from his teaching credential at San Jose State, stressed, "Education is the basic means to success," he said. "People can't get anywhere in the world by sitting and talking about what they could do...The important thing in school is not just running track and playing it cool, but hitting those books."[189] Smith's comments to the students were short. Tommie devoted the remainder of the extended 75-minute assembly to questions. The reporter noted:

```
When asked to explain his actions in Mexico City,
the sprinter commented, "I displayed the clenched
fist to let my people know that I am a black man and
proud of it...The black fist is a symbol of black
power. By this, I mean the black man is getting
into economics and getting a hand in business...[190]
```

A group of silver-haired men dressed in conservative suits stood along the side of the cafeteria. One of the men challenged, "If you don't like America, leave it!" And another chimed in, "You are a disgrace!" (Jack learned these were math and engineering professors from the local university who walked across the street to confront Tommie). Students whispered and squirmed – some snickered, and a few nodded in agreement. The tempo of banter quickened, and the temperature auditorium seemed even hotter when a parent barked, "You are an embarrassment to this country, and this is a waste of my son's time!" [191]

Elmeretta, a black student, later said, "I was sickened by the division and hostility generated between friends and people having degrees of sympathy for the cause."

ASB president Jeff Carter stood and addressed the crowd, "We are here to listen and to understand. You are here because you choose to be here." And then, to the angry father, he said, "There are other activities that your son can attend. No one is missing classes here." [192]

Smith addressed the crowd, "I am proud of what I did in Mexico, and I love America. You, I, and everyone in this room have an opinion, and we all have free speech. I just want to have a different America." Tommie looked at the audience and remarked, "When I came back [from Mexico City], my dad said, 'There are a lot of people who say you did a bad thing.' I said, 'Daddy, you've been working in the fields your whole life, picking cotton, being a cowboy, and you know there are some things that were done to you, and you knew it wasn't right. I put my hand up to say, let's work together, and let's fight racism. You are working for a man, but he needs to treat you like a man.' He looked at me and smiled and said, 'Well, you better keep talking.'" [193]

A student asked, "Are you prejudice against the white man?"

Smith replied, "I have more skepticism for the white man than for the black," and Tommie turned to Scotty sitting near him, "When I'm running on a team, everybody loves me, but when I cross the finish line, everybody goes their separate ways." [194]

Scotty nodded.

The assembly ended, the crowd dispersed, but its effects remained. The older, rigid generation continued complaining and took its grievances to the school board. The younger generation defended the movement and looked for hope. A Chico High school girl reflected, "I am ashamed of our past. We need to change now." A young man added, "He is a great man who should be respected and admired on and off the track." Rick, a senior, said, "He spoke sincerely...and he and several other black students were extremely effective in expressing the dilemma of the black in today's society." [195]

Two years after Tommie spoke at Chico High School, the black students, motivated to support the black experience on campus, organized the Black Student Union. They asked Jack to be the club's advisor. Jack continued in this role for nearly 30 years.

CHAPTER 21

The Donkey and the Jackass

"Coach, what should I do?" Jack asked.
Brutus simply replied, "Don't let him pass you." [196]

Jack's entry in the great race began at the Builder's Supply hardware store on the Skyway in Paradise. He waited for the cashier with a Hershey's bar in one hand and a bag of nails in the other when the man in line turned and greeted him with a broad smile, "Jack, it's good to see you again." It was Lou Logue, a local contractor, a sports booster, and a member of *E. Clampus Vitus,* a northern California mountain fraternity, "How would you like to run in the Donkey Derby?"

"What's a Donkey Derby?" asked Jack.

"It's how we celebrate Gold Nugget Days around here." Lou gave Jack a short course on local Paradise history. In 1859, a miner discovered a fifty-four-pound nugget in nearby Magalia. The miner carried the gold rock up the hill and out of the canyon on his donkey's back to the Dog Town Saloon. Paradise celebrates Gold Nugget Days every year. Festivities include a race where men and women lead a donkey loaded with fifty-four pounds of rocks three miles up a gravel logging road from Whiskey Flats along the river to Magalia on the upper ridge. The winner receives fifty dollars cash and a trophy. The *Pair-O-Dice 7-11 Chapter* of E. Clampus Vitus organizes the contest.

The Clampers are central to small-town festivities in the Sierra Nevada mountain communities. They are a hard-drinking fraternity that arrived in California during the Gold Rush era who parodied upstanding and conventional groups like the Elks and Masons. Clampers greeted each other with Latin-inspired titles – the *Noble Grand Humbug*, *Roisterous Iscutis*, or the *Grand Imperturbable Hangman*, and new officers are elected each year at the *Demotion Dinner*.

When a miner died, the group collected food and money for "the widow and any orphans who had been left behind." [197] A section of the March 16, 1853, New York Tribune shared news from the Angels Camp mining town on the other side of the country (the setting for Mark Twain's *Celebrated Jumping Frog of Calaveras County*). The paper reported six men murdered, a stabbing, a hanging, three more murders, a highway robbery, horse stealing, a jail escape, and a charitable donation:

> A society called the E. Clampus Vitus, at Murphy's donated the sum of $150* to a poor lady to enable her to establish a school at that place. This liberal act cannot be too highly commended. [198]

New Clampers pass through shrouded initiation rituals that are rumored to involve more drinking than anything else. Behind the beer, red long-johns, and providing aid to widows and orphans, E. Clampus Vitus restores and preserves California's Gold Rush history. Travelers will discover historical markers placed by the Clampers in parks and on the

---

* *Valued at nearly $5,000 today.*

sides of roads that depict notable events on that location. The New York Times details:

> With little more than mortar and their ever-pres-
> ent red shirts, the Clampers...have placed more
> than 1,000 bronze, wood, and granite plaques
> throughout California, from the remote stretches
> of coast to mining towns...in the foothills of
> the Sierra Nevada.[199]

Jack had seen the "Pair-O-Dice" Chapter of E. Clampus Vitus around town driving their fleet of an old hearse, a rusty fire truck, and a vintage school bus. Its members donned long red underwear, a vest, cowboy boots, and wide-brimmed hats. They pulled a jail-on-wheels and collected funds by snatching and incarcerating unsuspecting clean-shaven men for public humiliation until someone came to the rescue and purchased a Gold Nugget badge.

The Clampers erected two monuments in neighboring old Magalia. One plaque identifies the School House Bell, which today chimes from the Historic Magalia Community Church.* The other, located at the Old Depot,† remembers a railroad constructed in 1902 by the Diamond Match Company. However, it's a third monument dedicated by the Native Daughters of the Golden West that the Clampers celebrate each year with a Donkey Derby. This marker overlooks the jagged Feather River Canyon with its crumbling gold mines, echoing stories of hope, loss, and occasional fortune.

---

* *E. Clampus Vitus erected a third marker in 2019 on the first anniversary of the Camp Fire – a memorial to the 85 people who perished.*

† *The Old Depot was one of 17,000 structures destroyed in the 2018 Camp Fire.*

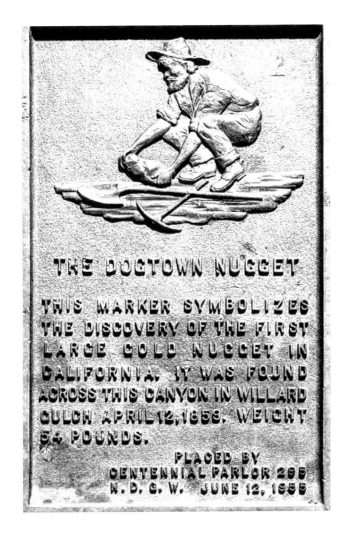

(Photo by author, 2020)

DOGTOWN NUGGET

THIS MARKER SYMBOLIZED THE DISCOVERY OF THE FIRST
LARGE GOLD NUGGET IN CALIFORNIA. IT WAS FOUND
ACROSS THE CANYON IN WILLARD GULCH APRIL 12, 1859.
WEIGHT 54 POUNDS.

The donkey that Lou had for Jack belonged to an 80-year-old miner, Jess Whitlow, who wanted his little burro in the competition, and Lou was looking for a way out of his promise to compete. Jack would be the scapegoat. "Sure," Jack replied. "What do I have to do?"

"Nothing," Lou responded. "Just show up at Whiskey Flats at eight a.m. on Saturday morning, and the donkey will be there ready to go."

That night, at the dinner table, Jack announced, "Your daddy's going to race in the Donkey Derby on Saturday."

Seven-year-old Bruce interjected, "Can I ride it?"

"When I get to the top of the hill, you can ride it," said Jack.

"And what do you know about donkeys?" asked Margo

"Absolutely nothing," admitted Jack.

Bryce, the precocious three-year-old, had an opinion. "Donkeys are *obstinate,*" repeating a word that Jack and Margo had used to describe him on occasion.

That week, Jack asked some students from farming families what they knew about donkeys. "Bring some carrots," a girl suggested.

Jack hadn't shaved in a week and looked ready to race. He sported a pair of tattered Convers All-Stars, track shorts, a loose button-down shirt, and a floppy red-white-and-blue hat. He met at the assembly point where the paved street met the gravel logging road. The nine racers loaded into the back of pickup trucks to be shuttled down the canyon switchbacks to the Whiskey Flats bridge.

Jack and "Little-Jack" Sharing a Snack

(Jack and Margo Yerman Collection)

The contestants lingered at the starting line. Lou and 80-year-old Mr. Whitlow introduced Jack to his namesake – *Little Jack,* a sad-eyed pint-sized burro. Jack learned that most of the donkeys in the race were *jennies,* or girl donkeys. And the male donkeys are called *jacks.* Homer was the biggest of all, the size of a horse, roped to a post and wildly eyeing the jennies mingling around.

Jack assessed the men and animals. "I'm in trouble," he thought and asked Mr. Whitlow for advice.

"Get to the top of the hill first and make it through the obstacle course," said the old-timer.

"Obstacles?" Jack questioned.

The Clampers built a course reminiscent of old mining days. After traversing the three-mile hill, contestants would guide the donkeys through an obstacle course of tires, railroad ties, and a canvas "mining tunnel" lined with empty cans rattling overhead.

A racer chimed in, "But it's the water that will get ya."

"Is that a problem?" Jack asked.

"Sure is...," said Bill, a contender with a *jennie* named *Rag Mop*. He paused to spit brown tobacco juice. "It's a pool with a black tarp, six inches deep, and the burros don't see the bottom, so they aint steppin' in. And that's the finish line."

Jack thought he should have done his homework before accepting this assignment. He leaned into his four-footed companion and whispered, "We need a plan."

The *Big Homer* nearby bellowed again, stomped, and pulled on its rope. "As long as we are in front of the big guy," Jack surmised, "we'll run to the finish line!"

The contestant lined up, and a Colt revolver signaled the competitors to action. *Homer* let out a bawl, and *Little Jack* and the *jennies* galloped forward. *Little-Jack's* pint-sized legs pounded on the gravel with Jack racing at his side. Jack wondered if he could keep up this pace when the *big jack* approached from behind. Panting, the beast chased after the jennies ahead and bellowed past Jack and his burrow.

Donkeys have a highly developed sense of self-preservation,[200] and Jack's little donkey, knowing that danger was now in front, halted. Jack watched the competitors with Chiquita, *Rag Mop, Ruben, End-of-Trail, Go-Get-Um, Flossy, Jennie,* and *Big Homer* disappear around the bend in a cloud of dust, leaving him and his donkey alone in the middle of the road. Donkeys have exceptional memories, and unbeknown to Jack, his little burro, who had raced this course before, had its own plan.

Jack pulled a carrot from his pocket. The donkey stepped forward, nibbled on the invitation, and advanced. Jack pulled on the rope. The donkey rebuffed. Jack wiggled the carrot in front of the burro's nose, and he moved. This time, Jack kept slack in the line and laid the rope over his shoulder. The donkey picked up the pace, and Jack matched the tempo. Soon it trotted, and Jack thinks *THIS IS WORKING!* The donkey then leaned into Jack and bumped him towards the edge of the road. Jacked realized *he's running me off a cliff.*

Jack shifted his position to the opposite side of the donkey. They rounded the switchback, and it again maneuvered to push him. Jack calculated the three-mile race to be more like five as the duo zigzagged up the mountain.

Jack arrived fifteen minutes behind the competition to a record crowd of 2,000 guffawing spectators. He and his burro approached the first obstacle when Bruce ran up, "Hurry, Daddy, no one can cross the water. You can still win!"

"Let's go!" smiled Jack. His little donkey, which had fought him up the mountain, picked up his ears, quickened its step, and overtook a donkey that refused to cross a white line on the road. The team trotted over the railroad ties and passed another competitor at the tunnel. It tiptoed through the tires and turned the corner to the mayhem of man, beast, and water.

Big Homer dragged its runner back and forth across the staging area. The jennies scattered to escape, and the screaming crowd dodged donkeys and men who pulled their animals to the water only to have the donkeys plant their front legs and refuse to advance. The reporter chronicled, "Several of the donkeys getting their forelegs into the water, managed to pull their drivers through the pool and away from the finish line." [201]

Jack looked at his little donkey. "It's our turn." The beast eyed the new-comers and pushed the little burro away from the jennies. Jack circled the area in front of the water with the little donkey dancing behind. Jack spun again with the big donkey in chase. The crowd squealed at the whirlwind of men a beast – Jack's wide-eyed donkey looked over its shoulder at the foaming creature in pursuit.

Jack pulled on his dizzy companion and, on the fourth or fifth turn, stepped into the trough. The cool water froze its stance, and the big jack that had turned to the jennies plowed into the back of Jack's animal. The chaos of men and animals tumbled in a splash. Jack heard the crowd cheering. He found his feet, stood, pulled on the rope, and stepped out on the other side with his donkey. A Clamper in red underwear hollered, "WE HAVE A WINNER!" *

The reporter wrote:

> Jack Yerman of Paradise...finally managed to cross the finish line in a comparatively slow time of 49 minutes, which was 15 minutes longer than 1969's winner.
>
> Coming in second was Wayne Josephson, driving "Jennie," and Larry Hanks, driving "Flossy" was third.
>
> There were nine entries in the race, but six failed to cross the finish line by going through the pool of water, even though some were dragged halfway through the hazard. [202]

---

* Jack (no. 3) and Little Jack navigate Donkey Derby obstacles:
  ▷ https://bit.ly/Donkey70

Jack stood triumphant on the grandstand between a pair of red-shirted Clampers to accept the fifty dollars in coins and a trophy replica of the gigantic nugget. Noting his name, the Clampers added a sentence to the award, pressed out on a Dymo Label Maker: *The first Jackass to lead a donkey up the hill.* To Bruce and Bryce's delight, Jack took his designated place in Paradise's Gold Nugget Parade that afternoon.[*]

The next few months became a year, and, in the tradition of great competitors, Jack decided to defend his championship. He asked if he could borrow *the little burro again,* but the now 81-year-old miner knowing he had a winner, had decided to enter the race. Jack asked his students if they knew of a donkey. The Wurlitzer brothers volunteered, "We have one on the ranch," and added, "but she doesn't know she's a donkey."

"What do you mean?" Jack asked.

"She's been around horses all her life, and we ride her like a horse jumping fences, running through streams and barrel racing. We call her Silver."

The brothers tell Jack they will take care of everything and deliver Silver to the starting area at the bottom of the canyon.

On race day, Jack was relieved not to see the screaming beast from the year before. The starting gun echoed off the canyon walls, and Silver trotted up the hill. At a quarter-mile, the duo caught up with a cowboy on a horse escorting the competition. Silver slowed to a walk, content to find an equine companion.

Jack pondered as he walked and then asked the cowboy, "Hey, could you gallop a little and see what my donkey does?"

The man nudged his horse forward with his boots, and Jack's donkey matched its pace. The team trotted up the hill with Jack running

---

[*] Jack in the 1970 Gold Nugget Parade:
     ▶ http://bit.ly/Parade70

alongside. To everyone's surprise, Jack and his donkey arrived at the obstacle course in twenty-five minutes. Jack calculated he had run a 10-minute mile up the gravel road for a thousand feet with a donkey. Silver walked over the railroad, negotiated the tires without hesitating, and marched through the tunnel. Silver bowed for a drink at the pool of cool water, and Jack nudged her forward. She placed a hoof and then another and pranced to the other side. It was a Donkey Derby world record. The Paradise Post recorded:

> Silver was the deciding factor in the race, running the course fast and pausing only a few seconds to go through the water barrier. [She] was timed at 33 minutes. [203]

The second, third, and fourth-place finishers eventually reached the top and crossed the water. The paper continued:

> Jess Whitlow, of Magalia, at the ripe age of 81 years, amazed the spectators with his endurance, placing fourth...[and] was given a rousing cheer for his performance. [204]

Bruce and Bryce ran to their father along with Margo, who carried the family's newest member. Blake Jefferson Yerman was one day shy of four weeks old, born in the early morning hours of March 27. When Blake arrived, the proud daddy carried the baby from the delivery room to where Margo's mother, Grandma Della, waited anxiously. She wrote in her journal, "Jack pulled back the blanket and said, 'Isn't he a beautiful baby boy - a new beautiful baby!'"

Jack held his newest son – his greatest prize.

Jack and Silver with Bruce, Bryce, and Blake

(Jack and Margo Yerman Collection)

CHAPTER 22

Irene

The problem is to set one's teeth against disappointment and carry on even more enthusiastically and determined for the races ahead. I know you will do this... Please remember me to your good mother and sweet sister.[205]

Coach Brutus Hamilton

Jack's mother visited Paradise each year and sat smoking in the same chair on the sunny front porch. She listened to the sound of family. Bruce, Bryce, and Blake flung the screen door open, "Hi, Grandma Yerman!" they shouted running outside to play, the aluminum screen door slamming back in place. The slender, white-haired grandmother watched through cat-eye glasses. She soaked in the morning's warmth, her lips in a relentless back-and-forth tic, chewing on something invisible between the puffs of cigarette smoke. She never asked a question nor responded to the kids with much more than one or two words and an occasional smile, but the boys believed she was content.

Irene's parents, Henry and Bertha Flamme, had moved their four daughters from South Dakota to northern California in the early 1920s. The Flammes may have sought the warmer climate and the fresh air like thousands of "lungers" diagnosed with consumption (tuberculosis). They had hoped Henry's condition would improve. The Flammes purchased a small peach farm in the unincorporated Tudor-Wilson area near Yuba City.

Henry Flamme

Bertha Flamme

The newspapers recorded social events and reported the family attending birthdays, weddings, and teaching Sunday school. Irene, the oldest of the girls, traveled to Yuba City for high school. She was smart, played on the girls' basketball team, was elected as Senior Class secretary and treasurer, and played a part in the seniors' end-of-the-year theatre performance. She had dreams and a plan. The Marysville Appeal-Democrat shared:

> **YUBA CITY. Aug. 11** — Miss Irene Flamme and Miss
> Lucia Inglerock, who graduated from the Yuba City
> Union High School with the class of '25, have
> enrolled at the University of California hospital
> for the three-year course in nursing. They left on
> Monday for San Francisco and will go into training
> at once. Both were popular here, and their friends
> wish them success in their chosen profession.[206]

Henry's deteriorating health may have played a part in Irene's plans to become a nurse. His persistent cough left his throat raw and dry, and his condition worsened. He lost weight. The family drove Henry to the Weimar Joint Tuberculosis Sanitarium in the Sierra Nevada Mountains 60 miles west of Tudor-Wilson. The taxpayer-funded hospital served patients unable to pay for private treatment. It advertised "fresh air, sunshine, good food, and bed rest" supplemented with "drugs and biochemicals for the alleviation of various distressing symptoms." The survival rate at the sanitarium was 50 percent.[207]

Henry died at the hospital on December 10, 1926. He was 49. Irene returned from her first semester of nursing school and sat with her mother, Bertha, and her sisters Gladys, Bertha, and Faye, at the funeral. The newspaper recognized Henry as a "well-known resident of the Tudor section," with many attending the service.[208]

Irene Yerman
University of California, San Francisco
Nursing School Graduate 1929
(Jack and Margo Yerman Collection)

Irene received her diploma in May 1929 and accepted a job at the modern 175-bed Sutter Hospital in Sacramento. She visited her mother and sisters, and the women tried to manage the farm, but eventually, Bertha had to sell the estate valued at $1,900. Gladys married a local farmer, and daughter Bertha married a boy from Yuba City. Faye, twelve years younger than Irene, worked alongside her mother when not at school. The social section of the newspaper recounted:

> **WILSON, Aug. 14.** Miss Irene Flamme, Mrs. Smith,
> and nephew of Sacramento drove up to spend Monday
> afternoon with Irene's mother, Mrs. Bertha
> Flamme... Mrs. Bertha Flame and daughter, Faye,
> are hulling almonds at the C.L. Adams Ranch.[209]

Gladys invited Irene to go horseback riding at her husband's family ranch. She introduced her sister to a farmhand, Loyd Charles Yerman. At 5'7", he was a sinewy man, good with horses and a rope, but often injured:

> Lloyd [sic] Yerman, 28, is recovering from minor
> injuries, which he received last week when thrown
> by a horse he was riding. Yerman was employed on
> the Harbinson property between Elkhorn and Knights
> Landing. He received bad bruises and is now recu-
> perating at his parents' home, Mr. and Mrs. I.C.
> Yerman, south of Woodland.[210]

Loyd and Irene were older than others dating at the time, and Irene had a university education while Loyd had completed the 8th-grade. Growing up, Irene was diligent, careful, and methodical, while Loyd was carefree and rebellious. At 18, he stole a car and took two friends on a 260-mile joy ride from Central to Southern California.[211] Maybe Loyd seemed exciting to Irene, or perhaps she liked nurturing his injuries, or maybe they simply gravitated to each other. Loyd, 32, and Irene, 28, eloped to Reno on November 15, 1935. They announced the marriage to their families the next day.[212]

During the Great Depression, states drafted laws prohibiting married women from working to make room for unemployed men.[213] While nursing remained a woman's occupation and outside of a man's professional lane, the Sacramento County Hospital Medical Superintendent affirmed, "I desire to replace all married nurses, but I want to be certain the single women who take the positions are as efficient as the ones they replace."[214] Sutter Hospital, where Irene worked, was the same. Married, Irene could not keep her job, and Loyd was again injured and could not work:

WOODLAND (Yolo Co.), Jan 4. Lloyd [sic] Yerman of Woodland, employed by Hughes and Holmes, was given treatment here Saturday for an injured right leg and body and cuts and bruises after a horse he was riding stumbled and fell on him Friday afternoon at Wheatland. Mr. Yerman is able to be about, but will be unable to work...[215]

Loyd with a Lasso

Irene learned she was pregnant, and the newlyweds had little choice but to move in with her mother while Loyd recovered from his injuries.[216] Loyd and Irene bounced between Mama Bertha's home in Tudor-Wilson and Loyd's parents in Woodland until a blond-haired, beautiful blue-eyed little girl, Kathleen Irene Yerman, was born on August 20, 1936, at the hospital in Yuba City.

Loyd landed work in Oroville to the north. Irene followed him, and they lived at the Auto Park, a campground* on the edge of town and nestled in a grove of giant oaks on the banks of the Feather River for nearly two years during the Great Depression with other workers as neighbors, some in trailers and the others in tents. The Auto Park had electric lighting, showers, bath facilities, and complimentary wood for the outdoor cookstoves and ranges.[217] Its shady canopy and refreshing waters provided comfort during the hot summer while little Kathy explored with her mother the world of songbirds, cicadas, and wildlife along the river.

Doctors prescribed morphine to dull Loyd's pain, and when the drug was unavailable, he turned to alcohol. Prohibition, the law forbidding the production, transportation, and sale of alcohol in the 1920s and 30s, ended in California in 1934. Saloons came out of hiding, and legal liquor flooded the market.[218] Loyd drank more on paydays and he drank before driving:

> Lloyd [sic] Charles Yerman, whose automobile was involved in a collision on the Oroville-Quincy Road with a car driven by Mrs. Mary M. Bird Tuesday, changed a previous plea of not guilty to one of guilty in the Oroville justice court today on a drunken-driving charge. He was fined $150 by Justice of the Peace Harry. S. Hills.[219]

With twenty-five percent of the country out of work, living at the Auto Camp seemed ordinary, and Loyd accepted jobs where he could, but the hard liquor encumbered his reactions, perhaps contributing to continued mishaps:

---

* *Now Highway 70.*

Lloyd [sic] Yerman of 1616 Marysville Road [the Auto Camp] hurt his wrist yesterday when a horse he led pulled back on the rope. Yerman had the rope wrapped around his wrist, and the horse suddenly became frightened and jerked on the rope. Dr. E A. Kusel treated the fractured wrist. It will be five or six weeks before Yerman can use his arm.[220]

Irene discovered she was pregnant again but did not immediately turn to family. Summers along the river could be pleasant, and Oroville had established a Relief Committee to help the unemployed find work at the camp:

Men with families, who receive help, work seven hours a day for $1 grocery orders. In the last three weeks, more than 90 needy residents have been able to earn the grocery orders by working on improvements being made in the various park areas... [The men] are all married, have families, and need your help... At present, four fireplaces are being built at the auto park so that residents may hold picnics there.[221]

Loyd recovered and found work in town.[222*] Summer yielded to fall, which faded into winter, and Irene and Kathy moved to Tudor-Wilson for the final weeks of her pregnancy. When the contractions commenced, Irene's sister, Faye, drove her 45 miles north to the County Hospital in Oroville. On Sunday, February 5, 1939, the sun warmed the morning's frost and welcomed a healthy John Loyd Yerman to the world. Loyd senior was absent, confined at the County Jail probably for drinking. Irene asked Faye to take her to the

---

*   *"Loyd Yerman, who lives at a local auto camp, reported to city police theft of a leather jacket, taken while he was working near Municipal Auditorium. He left the coat halfway between the Gardella Theater and the levee, he said." Oroville Mercury Register, 9 December 1938.*

downtown jail. The deputy escorted Loyd to the window where he could see Irene and baby "Jack."

Irene divorced Loyd before Jack's second birthday. In 1941, Loyd submitted the required Army registration, and when asked to share contact information of someone who would always know his whereabouts. He could have shared his parent's address, or a sibling's, or maybe someone he had worked for, but he scribbled, "*Kathleen Yerman at 122 Fourth Street in Woodland.*" She was five years old.

The Army inducted Loyd at the age of 38 in September 1942. He reported for duty in October and in December was discharged for a "disability not in the line of duty." The doctor recorded a "Chrondrectomy," the removal of cartilage. Loyd received a small army pension which he spent on alcohol. Jack remembers taking a bus to Sacramento with his mother to search the flophouses along the river where vagrants congregated. Jack held his mother's hand, sidestepping scattered liquor bottles, marching up and down rickety stairs, and knocking on the doors of flea-infested flats looking for his father and the money he owed. Loyd never visited, never paid, and was never a father.

As World War II advanced, local hospitals faced a nursing shortage. Irene took the night shift at the Woodland Clinic. A taxi picked her up each evening while Grandma Flamme and the children prepared for bed. Jack and Kathy returned from play at dinnertime, which was sometimes bread and milk when the money was low. Grandma would say, "Jack, your mother has something to say to you," and he would stand before Irene, waiting for her to speak. "You need to get out of your school shirt and jeans before you play!" she admonished.

Irene's sister, Bertha Harris, passed away in May of 1963, and in November, Irene lost the anchor of her life, her mother. Jack and Margo drove to Woodland from Santa Clara to check on Irene and found her in her living room in a cloud of tobacco smoke. She had covered the windows with newspaper, sat in the dark, and lit her cigarette with a twenty-dollar bill. The doctors at the clinic referred Irene to the Highland Psychiatric Ward in Oakland for a little-understood wonder treatment:

> ...when one begins to contemplate the futility of living, it's time to see a doctor. Electroshock may be very much in order...[EST] frightens a patient no more than having a tooth pulled...[and why it] succeeds in aborting depression is also a mystery, but in a typical depression, one can expect dramatic relief with three or four treatments, and the average patient will hardly need more than six or eight treatments to be pulled out of the illness.[223]

Although it would have been an easy commute for Jack and Margo from Santa Clara to Oakland, visitors were not allowed. Patients waited for treatment, some reading, some playing solitaire, but most just sat. An orderly motioned towards Irene. She stood, wearing one of the two simple dresses she had packed, and he escorted her to a separate room with rows of beds, fifteen altogether, all of which contained unconscious patients who had just received treatment. "It's not pleasant to watch," Irene had read, "but the patient loses consciousness and doesn't feel a thing."

Irene removed her shoes and laid down in her dress on the bed. She noticed the small box on a mobile cart near her head. She felt a hand probe her hair for bobby pins while another nurse swabbed a sticky paste on a pair of smooth black knobby objects connected to wires running from the box.

"Open your mouth," instructed a nurse. Irene complied to receive the rubber wedge pushed between her teeth. She heard another ask, "Ready,

Doctor?" He nodded, the nurse touched the knobby instruments to Irene's temples, and the doctor pulled a switch on the box.

Electricity shot through the wires, and into her brain. Irene's world went black, her eyes shut, her body stiffened, her forehead wrinkled, and her fists clenched tight. Seconds later, her body seized and shook. The doctor turned off the current, and the nurse pulled the rubber wedge from the patient's mouth.

Irene uttered a deep, gurgling rattle, grunted loudly, and her eyes fluttered. Her pupils had rolled to the top of her head. The nurses turned Irene to her side, strapped her into bed, and left her to rest. Fifteen minutes later, Irene stirred. A nurse freed her from the restraints and told her to follow the others. Irene obeyed, walked with deliberate steps to another room, and sat down to a plate of toast and cup of coffee. Her senses slowly returned between the sips of coffee, and a painful headache set in. A doctor gave her two aspirin and told her she would soon feel better. Her treatment for the day was over. Irene repeated this routine during the next two weeks, feeling better after each treatment until discharged.[224*]

Jack visited his mother at home in Woodland and explored a family box. He found a hand-written evaluation from Irene's nursing school, "She's quite intelligent," he read, "but a little odd." The words on paper affirmed his experiences with his mother. He reached for a vinal record sitting near the turntable he had gifted her when he was in school. Irene liked music, and she played her small collection while she tied the hundreds of darns that grew to intricate doilies and curtains after weeks of work.

---

* *Merla Zellerbaack, a San Francisco writer in the 1960s, questioned the claims of shock treatments. Much of this text is based on her description of a woman that she had observed in treatment.*

In 1965, Jack's father walked off the street into a Sacramento hospital. He collapsed on the waiting room floor, where he died. Loyd was 61. The obituary recognizes Kathy and Jack but makes no mention of Irene. The Yolo County Veterans honored his one-month active duty at the graveside service with taps and an old soldier firing three volleys into the air representing duty, honor, and country. The Veterans paid for his tombstone and spelled his name wrong with two "Lls."

Irene retired in 1972 after thirty years of night shifts, and the Woodland Clinic honored her in the hospital cafeteria during lunch. Jack was there. Her colleagues paused from treating patients to attend the ceremony while a physician gave a short speech and handed Irene an envelope. Inside, she found tickets for a trip to Hawaii. Her colleagues applauded and congratulated her, and then it was back to work.

Irene traveled to the Aloha State alone.

CHAPTER 23

Mercy

Forgive each one his base desire;
Thy Wisdom guide, They Love inspire
Thy Blessings, Lord [225]

Coach Brutus Hamilton

A long-distance phone call from Paradise to Woodland in 1975 cost about the same as a tank of gas, so Jack and Margo made few calls beyond the county's border. Still, Margo had a strong sense of family and wrote letters to Irene, keeping her connected to Jack and the boys. Irene always wrote back. Margo handed Jack a letter addressed to him. He read a few lines, stopped, and looked at Margo. "What!"

> *Dearest Margo,*
> *I have been taking lessons with the missionaries and will be baptized. I hope you and Jack will be there, and I would like Jack to baptize me...*

Jack reread the words. He had been baptized into the Church of Jesus Christ of Latter-day Saints fifteen years prior and had served as a Cub Scout leader, a Sunday School Teacher, and was an Elder, but he never thought to share his faith with his mother. She was addicted to coffee and tobacco, two habits she would have to give up as a Mormon, and she had never had a real conversation with him about anything.

Jack telephoned his mother, and Margo talked to the missionaries. They learned that the two white-shirt-clad young men had marched from door to door on a warm August day without success. They were hot, tired, hungry, and discouraged. The boys returned to the car, flopped into the seats, and loosened their ties. The senior companion turned the ignition key, and the engine came to life. The missionaries navigated through the neighborhood, turned onto Fourth Street, and the junior companion sat up, "Stop the car!"

"What?"

"Stop the car! We're going to knock on one more door."

His companion pulled over and looked at a street of tired, older homes, "OK, which one?" he asked.

The Elder sat for a moment and pointed to a small white house on the right. "That one!" he said, pulling his tie back into place.

The pair knocked on the door. Irene answered and two cheerful young men greeted her. "Hello. We're missionaries from the Church of Jesus Christ of Latter-day Saints."

Irene knew her grandsons would be missionaries someday and welcomed the pair into her home. She offered them a cold glass of water and a plate of Lorna Doone shortbread cookies. The young ministers sat at the kitchen table and explained they were on a two-year hiatus from work and school to teach about Christ. Irene's Bible lay on the table, and the three shared favorite scriptures. Irene invited the missionaries to return for several weeks, and somehow, she reached deep into her character, not unlike Jack's world-class training discipline, to find the resolve to give up her beloved tobacco and coffee, and she asked to be baptized.

Jack and Margo loaded the boys into the van on a sunny October Saturday in 1975. The pair of missionaries accompanying Irene and Jack's sister, Kathy, met them at the chapel in Sacramento. Irene wiggled a piece of hard candy in her mouth, replacing the cigarettes. Kathy, who was cheerful and talkative by nature, seemed extra exuberant. Kathy's whispers reverberated across the room, and when Margo's sister, Karen, sang, "I Know that My Redeemer Lives," the same hymn she had sung years earlier at Jack's baptism, Kathy doted, "That *soooo* beautiful – isn't she lovely? You are magnificent, Karen!" Kathy had spent little time in any church, and Margo ignored the impropriety while Jack focused on his mother.

Dressed in white, Jack escorted Irene to the baptismal font. Taking his mother's arm, he stepped down the stairs and into the tepid waist-deep water. Kathy stood and squealed, "Jackie, you be careful with my mom! Be careful, Jackieee!" – the name she had used with Jack when he was little. Jack recited the prayer and dipped his mother into the water. Baptism is sacred, and two witnesses must confirm its accuracy. Jack missed a word and needed to perform the ordinance again. Kathy called out, "Jackie, be careful! Be careful with my mom."

Jack suppressed his agitation, enacted the ordinance again, and when Irene surfaced, the witness informed Jack that she had not gone entirely under the water. He would need to do it again. "What's the matter, Jackie? My mother can only take so much of this!" She continued, "Jackie, you do it right this time. It's OK, Mom; Jackie will take care of you," she called out. Jack ignored his sister, recited the prayer, and pushed his mother deep into the water. She came up, he got a nod from the witnesses, and escorted his mother up the steps. Phil Pearson, Jack's friend from high school, pulled Jack aside, patted him on the back, and pulled the tension from the room observing, "That's the first play-by-play baptism I've attended!"

After the service, Jack helped Irene and Kathy into the van. Kathy maneuvered to sit and fell between the seats, landing on her bottom, giggling. Jack pulled her up, looked at her, and the morning's calamity came into focus. Kathy had been drinking.

Kathy had enjoyed Jack's fame, in part, because others noticed her when in his glow. Jack found his confidence on the playground, in sports, at church, and Phil was a good friend. Kathy had a more challenging time in her youth. Although newspapers from the era report Kathy winning a downtown holiday turkey by saying *Merry Christmas* to the right person at the right time,[226] and performing in a fashion show with several other girls,[227] Kathy had to work to be like her friends. Jack remembers Kathy laying in the back yard in a bikini, oiling her skin, and soaking up the sun to stay on par with her peers going to the beach. When the girls got together after the holiday, Kathy shared the details of her invented vacation. It was difficult for Kathy to fit in at school. The parties, the boys, and the alcohol became her answer for acceptance, and as she matured, jobs replaced the parties, husbands replaced the boys, but her attachment to alcohol remained.

Margo continued writing to Irene and reminded the boys to pen a note to their grandmother. Letters evolved to cassette tapes. Margo narrated the play-by-play into the microphone with Jack and the boys wrestling in the background, or she set the recorder near the piano while Bruce and Bryce hammered on the keys. Blake shared his stories in a gravelly little voice, and everyone talked about Brook, the new baby born September 13, 1976. Jack gloated a message to his mother on the tape:

The baby has done a first. She turned from her back to tummy, and she loves to touch and taste everything, which makes her slobber. She's a curious baby – a happy baby – a healthy baby. She's a lot of fun to have around. We are blessed.

Irene's letters conveyed that Kathy had moved out of her apartment and in with her. Jack telephoned Kathy to learn more. "Mom needs me," she said. "I can take care of her."

Jack admonished, "Kathy, you need to promise that you will go to AA. You can't be the problem. You can't drink and take care of mom."

"I'm not going to AA," Kathy retorted, "I've beat this before, and I'll do it again!"

Kathy's childhood experience must have been like his, and Irene likely told Kathy that she, too, needed to leave after high school. Kathy had found her exit ticket when she married Edward Gonsalves in 1956. She was 19, and he was 22. The marriage lasted 14 months.

Kathy married Charles Muller two years after the divorce. Chuck was handsome, hardworking, and a good baseball player. Seven and a half months later, little Charles was born, followed by Kenneth in another two years. The Muller's bought a home in the growing City of Davis and enjoyed meat and potato dinners, watching football on TV, playing with Tonka Trucks and riding bicycles. The boys suited up for Little League games. Chuck was their coach, and Kathy sat with the moms in the bleachers. Her son Kenny remembers his mother as a skilled homemaker and a good mom when she wasn't drinking. She decorated the home, made delicious meals, laughed easily, played with her miniature poodle, and loved her boys. Still, she yearned for attention, and everyday challenges swelled into disasters. Kenny believes she coped by drinking, and Jack observed she used alcohol to turn attention back to her. She and Chuck divorced in 1975, and the boys lived with their father.

Kathy married Vernon Wesley Chisum on Halloween Day in a Reno Wedding Chapel in 1976. Kathy and "Walter," as he called himself, drove to Paradise to meet Jack's family. Bruce remembers the shiny new red Malibu pulling up to the Camellia Drive home and a beaming Kathy introducing her braggadocios millionaire husband to an astonished Jack and Margo. Twelve-year-old Bruce shook the man's hand, but he did not trust him. Cousin Kenny later said he was a crook. Chism claimed to be a crop-duster pilot and owned airplanes. He had big plans. Jack learned he bought the Malibu with a loan in Kathy's name.

Chism moved into the tiny 122 Fourth Street house with Kathy and Irene, and by the spring of 1977, they had moved Irene to a senior care facility to treat her chronic angina and increasing chest pain. It was too late when Jack learned that Kathy and Walter had pilfered Irene's meager funds, sold her belongings, and thrown away Irene's journals and Jacks' childhood box of memories. Jack and Margo visited Irene. She stared at the ceiling disheartened and in pain, responding to Jack's inquiries in one or two-word sentences.

Jack's mother died in the nursing home on August 7, 1977, at 70. The doctor recorded heart failure on the death certificate, but the orderly reported that she was found with a plastic bag over her head. Irene had left a note, "*I believe in God, my faith, and give my special love to the grandchildren.*"

CHAPTER 24

The Victory Lap

When a runner achieves athletic immortality by finally accomplishing this goal, his name alone will be written in the record books, but like the scaling of Everest, his achievement should be considered a team effort.[228]

Coach Brutus Hamilton

The Collegiate All-American strolled into Edwards Stadium for practice. Jack wore a loose white t-shirt, blue practice shorts, black canvas Chuck Taylors, and his running spikes dangling from his hand. The fragrance of freshly cut grass was a nice contrast to the musty lecture rooms. Berkeley attracted the brightest in the country, courses were intense, and Jack blew off stress from the hours of study. Jack sauntered to the high jump to banter with the jumpers. He rolled over the bar a couple of times, landing in the sawdust pit. Jack brushed himself off. "Good thing I'm not a jumper!" he laughed, unaware that Coach Hamilton watched.

"Jack! Come talk to me for a minute," called out the coach.

Jack picked up his spikes and jogged over to Brutus Hamilton. "Yes, sir." Coach Hamilton observed a bit of a swagger in Jack's relaxed demeanor.

"What are you doing, Jack? Are you here to practice?"

"Coach, this is an easy week – I'm going to win." Nearby San Jose State and a local track club would host Saturday's meet.

Brutus was a quiet man and had become a father figure to Jack. The coach looked at his young runner. He leaned in close, and his voice softened, "There will be runners who see *this* as the *biggest* race in their career. They will compete against *Jack Yerman*, a world-ranked athlete, and tell their children about this race. Would you dishonor your competition by running less than your very best?"

A hint of shame grew from Jack's belly. He pulled his eyes from the man he respected more than any other. "Yes, sir," he said. Jack exchanged his Converse for his spikes, joined his teammates, and hit the interval training harder than anyone. In San Jose, Jack crossed the tape in a world-class time, winning by ten meters, and Coach Hamilton's insights would prove prophetic.

A hometown reporter interviewed Jack in 1984 for an article titled Quiet Pride:

Jack Yerman has never made a movie or a television commercial. He has never been on a box of Wheaties, and he's a household name only in Woodland and perhaps parts of Berkeley, where he played running back on Cal's 1959 Rose Bowl team. But Jack Yerman, who has lived in Paradise since 1968, is only one of 155 living Americans who earned the Olympic gold medal. Yerman's great moment in sports came in the summer of 1960 in the Rome Olympics when he helped the U.S. mile relay team beat Germany for the gold on the Stadio Olimpico track.

For the record, Yerman ran the then-fastest first leg in Olympic history, 46.2, to put the U.S. foursome in front to stay. Earl Young, Glenn Davis, and

Otis Davis followed Yerman's lead to give the Yanks
a three-yard victory of the Germans in 3:02.2.
That was [1960] in what Yerman only half-jok-
ingly refers to as "the last of the old-fashioned
Olympics." [229]

The reporter shared details of Jack's family, of a 21-year-old Bruce who
may have followed in his footsteps except for a radicle knee surgery, and
Bryce, a gifted students who chose to climb vertical cliffs rather than run
in circles, and middle-schooler, Blake, the "eater of the family" who played
soccer and sometimes joined Jack for sprints, and Brook, "a young charmer
who walks about the house beating her father to punchlines…" The journal-
ist continued:

Margo is a disarming keeper of the straight record
in the Yerman home. At first meeting, she told
this reporter, "Hi, I'm the Beast. They live here
with me." But Margo, like Jack, has her serious
moments. While Jack will talk about keeping his
gold medal in his dresser, she will explain his
apparent lack of enthusiasm. "I think he's made
a conscientious effort not to make a thing of it,"
she said. "You can't live your life on something
you did 24 years ago."

Not that Jack is devoid of pride. When one mar-
vels about his running back-to-back [400's] of
46.0 and 46.3 in the 1960 Olympic Trials, he
will add that "they were run within an hour and
a half of each other." He also will reveal that
he trained only two hours a day back then because
of a hectic schedule, compared to the six and
eight-hour sessions typical of today's world-
class athletes.

He also is quick to stress the importance of being
lucky, as well as good. "You have to be at the
right place at the right time," Jack insists. "Look
at Rink Babka. He was the No. 1 discus thrower in
the world, and he never got a gold medal. You have
to be lucky"... [230]

The 1984 Olympics provided the backdrop for Jack's interview. The
Soviets had announced a boycott of the Olympics in Los Angeles in retalia-
tion of the U.S. embargo of the Games four years prior in Moscow to punish
the Soviets for the invasion of Afghanistan.[231] Jack called the '84 Olympics
"Politically trashed" but noted the government has often used international
sports for political gain.[232]

The University of California inducted Jack into the Hall of Fame in 1994.
The cohort included former coaches and athletes who excelled in rugby,
tennis, swimming, football, volleyball, basketball, and track.[*] A thousand
guests gathered at the Marriott Hotel in Berkley for dinner. The Master of
Ceremony introduced each athlete with a video followed by a short talk from
the inductee.

Sylvie Monnet, a Swiss volleyball player and the youngest in the group,
impressed Jack. She was from a small village in the Alps and spoke halt-
ing English when she arrived as a new student. She learned quickly, found

---

*   *University of California Hall of Fame Inductees 1994: Gerald Stratford (Tennis
    1924-26), Graham Smith (Swimming 1979-82), Ron Rivera (Football 1980-83),
    Paul Larson (Football 1952-54), Miles "Doc" Hudson (Rugby Coach 1938-
    74), Larry Friend (Basketball 1955-57), Pete Cutino (Water Polo Coach 1963-
    88), Sylvie Monnet (Volleyball 1980-83), Jack Yerman (Track & Field 1958-60,
    Football 1957-58).*

her niche, and became a three-year Academic All-American, the only All-American from the *Cal* women's volleyball program in twenty years. She loved the school, her education, and her sport. She currently played on the Swiss National and Olympic volleyball teams.

Jack was the final inductee, and the event culminated. He and Margo mingled in conversation and memories. A man and his adult son caught Jack's attention and introduced themselves. "You are the reason I married my wife," said the man.

Jack was curious and a little worried.

"I loved going to track meets with my father growing up," said the man, "and in 1960, I took a girl on a first date to the *Cal-Stanford* dual meet. *Cal* would win an event and then Stanford, and it came down to who could take the mile relay. I pointed to *Jack Yerman* and told Janice, 'Exciting things happened when Yerman runs, and he's anchoring the relay. Your team was ten meters behind when you took the baton," said the man to Jack. "You sprinted the first curve, gained ground on the backstretch, and as you raced around the last turn just off the shoulder of the Stanford runner, Janice bolted from the top of the bleachers and ran track-side screaming, *Run like hell you son of a bitch*! You won, and I knew she'd be the one I'd marry."

Jack and Margo chuckled at the story when the attractive six-foot-two, blond volleyball player Sylvie introduced herself. "I'm glad to meet you," she said to Jack. "I came to Berkeley because of you."

"Me?" said Jack, surprised. She was a student at *Cal* two decades after Jack and Margo.

Ms. Monnet shared details about her small village and becoming a national volleyball player. "When I was eighteen, my father put me in the car and drove me to the airport in Zurich. I cried when I saw the plane waiting to go to America. 'Why do I have to go to Berkeley, father?'"

He answered, "Because that is where Jack Yerman went to school."

She explained that when her father was young, he had seen Jack run with the American team in Europe. He followed Jack in the papers and watched how he conducted himself on the track. Jack thinks he may have been one of the hundreds of fans who approached the Americans for autographs. Jack signed dozens of programs and engaged with the enthusiasts' broken English. Mr. Monnet followed Jack's career and read about his wins, losses, tenacity, ethic, and education.

"Thank you, Mr. Yerman, for making an impression on my father."

More than three decades prior, when Jack upset the competition for a dramatic 400-meter victory at the Olympic Trials, and still gasping for air, he told the reporter, "Coach Hamilton is the best in the business…, and I ran just as he told me. He's 90 percent of my success." [233]

Bruce Hamilton Yerman with Coach Brutus Hamilton
(Jack and Margo Yerman Collection)

The coach, Olympian, poet, philosopher, husband, father, and friend had bequeathed a legacy to his young athletes. Brutus' words lingered with Jack well beyond the track, supplanting the quiet and comforting voice, "*Your time will come*," that he once had as a boy:

If I am remembered at all, it will be for the "little things." None of the several contributions which I thought rather pertinent at the time will be remembered a week beyond my departure: but some nonsense which I have concocted or been party to may earn me a tiny little footnote in the history of my time.[234]

Coach Brutus Hamilton

EPILOGUE

Margo died on May 24, 2014, of complications from multiple myeloma, a cancer of the plasma cells. Jack devoted his final days with her to feeding her soup and brightening her spirits with his silly sense of humor. Before she died, she gave Jack permission to buy his dream car that he had pestered her about for years. And, she suggested he marry again. Two weeks later, Jack purchased a new red Corvette Stingray, and in July of 2018, he married his new sweetheart, Carol Mattern of Paradise.

On November 8, 2018, Jack and Carol received an urgent call while visiting friends in Puerto Rico. A raging wildfire approached the Town of Paradise three-thousand miles away. Everyone was evacuating. They called a friend to rescue Brady, Carol's dog, and retrieve Jack's gold medal. Jack, Carol, and 15,000 families lost their homes that day in the devastating Camp Fire. Little Brady and the gold medal escaped the destruction.

Jack and Carol rebuilt their home and returned to Paradise in 2021.

Jack and Carol
July 21, 2018
(Photo by Maya Yerman-Sanchez)

SOURCES

1. Adapted from correspondence from student sent to Jack Yerman.

2. G.M. Walton, Beyond Winning; *The Timeless Wisdom of Great Philosopher Coaches*, Champaign: Leisure Press, 1992.

3. E. Martin, "Here's how much housing prices have skyrocketed over the last 50 years in every US state," 27 June 2017. [Online]. Available: https://www.cnbc.com/2017/06/27/how-much-housing-prices-have-increased-since-1940-in-every-state.html#:~:text=The%20median%20value%20for%20a,or%20the%20equivalent%20of%20%2436%2C700. [Accessed 24 May 2021].

4. IISRP, "Elastomers Shaping the Future of Mankind," [Online]. Available: http://www.iisrp.com/WebPolymers/00Rubber_Intro.pdf. [Accessed 7 August 2011].

5. B. Hamilton, "To Jack Yerman, July 11, 1957," in *The Worlds of Brutus Hamilton*, Palo Alto, CA: Tafnews Press, 1975, p. 24.

6. B. Hamilton, "From Remarks Delivered at Marin Sports Injuly Conference March 10, 1962," in *The Worlds of Brutus Hamilton*, Palo Alto, CA: Tafnews Press, 1975, p. 58.

7. A. Dumas, *The Count of Monte Cristo*, E-Book: Barrns and Nobel, 2010.

8. G.M. Walton, Beyond Winning; *The Timeless Wisdom of Great Philosopher Coaches*, Champaign: Leisure Press, 1992.

9. D. Ives, "Crippled Bears Fire-Up for First Test," *The Daily Californian,* p. 4, 19 September 1958.

10. N. Maxwell, "Teeter Totter Twins May Tackle World's Record," *The Daily Californian,* p. 2, 26 March 1958.

11. The Greater Lansing Area Sports Hall of Fame, "Sam Williams," 1982. [Online]. Available: https://lansingsportshalloffame.org/people/sam-williams/. [Accessed 18 May 2021].

12. G. S. Alderton, "Spartains Set for California's First Invasion," *Lansing State Journal,* p. 24, 26 September 1958.

13. TK Legacy Trading Card.

14. "Jack Yerman Speeds 36 Yards to Touchdown, "*Oakland Tribune*, p. 62, 12 October 1958.

15. *The Daily Californian,* October 1958.

16. B. Hamilton, "To Lee Covington, April 7, 1958," in *The Worlds of Brutus Hamilton*, Los Altos, CA: Tafnews Press, 1975, p. 29.

17. "Athletes Americains a Lausanne," *Feuille D'avis de Lausanne,* p. 27, 27 Juin 1958.

18. D.P. Martin, *Meeting USA, 1958.*

19. AP, "Yerman Wins for U.S. in Swiss Meet," *Oakland Tribune,* p. 45, 2 July 1958.

20. C. Tonelli, "Seibert, Yerman: View on the Olympics," *The Daily Californian,* 23 September 1960.

21. G.M. Dessena, "Un 800-record mancaato ed Altre cosa ruiscite," *La Gazzetta dello Sort,* pp. 1-2, 8 luglio 1958.

22. B. Hamilton, "To Mr. Avery Brundage, November 28, 1953," in *The Worlds of Brutus Hamilton*, Palo Alto, Tafnews Press, 1975, p. 81.

23. AP, "U.S. Trackmen Leave For Russia Tomorrow," *Bakersfield Californian,* pp. 18, 19 July 1958.

24. D. Marannis, The Olympics that Changed the World, New York: Simon & Schuster, 2008.

25. L. Chong, "Intourist, shorn of its Stalinist past, plans LSE listing," 10 October 2006. [Online]. Available: https://www.thetimes.co.uk/article/intourist-shorn-of-its-stalinist-past-plans-lse-listing-2gbrvlsfs5q. [Accessed 18 May 2021].

26. N. Lenin, "Socialism and Religion," Lenin Internet Arcive (2000) Public Domain, 12 December 1905. [Online]. Available: https://www.marxists.org/archive/lenin/works/1905/dec/03.htm. [Accessed 18 May 2021].

27. D. Marannis, *The Olympics that Changed the World*, New York: Simon & Schuster, 2008.

28. F. Litsky, 8 August 2010. [Online]. Available: http://www.nytimes.com/2010/08/20/sports/20connolly.html. [Accessed 18 May 2021].

29. Evergreen Athletic Fund, "Harold Connolly," n.d. [Online]. Available: http://hammerthrow.org/about-us/harold-connolly/. [Accessed 18 May 2021].

30. F. Litsky, 8 August 2010. [Online]. Available: http://www.nytimes.com/2010/08/20/sports/20connolly.html. [Accessed 18 May 2021].

31. I. Willoughby, "Olga Fikotova-Connolly: 1956 Olympic champion dubbed "traitor" in communitst Czechoslovakia over romance with US athlete," Chech Radio, 1 May 2008. [Online]. Available: https://english.radio.cz/olga-fikotova-connolly-1956-olympic-champion-dubbed-traitor-communist-8596615. [Accessed 18 May 2021].

32. Prague Post, "The Golden Girl," 20 Dec 2006. [Online]. Available: http://www.praguepost.com/archivescontent/2813-thegolden-girl.html. [Accessed 15 October 2012].

33. S. Duguid, "Olga Fikotiva, Czechoslovakia: Olga and Harold Connolly thawed the cold war a litte when they found love," Financial Times Magazine, 8 June 2012. [Online]. Available: https://www.ft.com/content/a194b7a2-adfc-11e1-bb8e-00144feabdc0. [Accessed 18 May 2021].

34. I. Willoughby.

35. S. Duguid.

36. I. Willoughby.

37. Rafer Johnson," n.d. [Online]. Available: http://www.myblackhistory.net/Rafer_Johnson.htm. [Accessed 18 May 2021].

38. AP, "U.S. Trackmen Leave For Russia Tomorrow," *Bakersfield Californian,* p. 18, 19 July 1958.

39. D. Bloom, "Yerman Hands to Courney & Hail the Conquerors," *Woodland Daily Democrat,* p. Sports News, 2 August 1958.

40. R. Musel, "Moscow Results Leave Everbody Happy," *The Bakersfield Californian,* p. 25, 29 July 1958.

41. I. Willoughby.

42. I. Willoughby.

43. Prague Post.

44. Prague Post.

45. G.M. Walton.

46. "Spy Trial Hears of Blackmail of Envoy," *Oakland Tribune*, p. E 3, 5 October 1961.

47. *Parade*, p. 12, 7 January 1962.

48. B. Hamilton, "To Kathy Buchanan [Former Secretary in the Athletic Office)," in *The Worlds of Brutus Hamilton*, Los Angeles, 1975.

49. "Slate Program," *The Daily Californian*, vol. 20, p. 1, 3 March 1958.

50. "Slate Program," *The Daily Californian*, vol. 20, p. 1, 3 March 1958.

51. Editor, "Slate Strikes Again," *The Daily California*, p. 8, 11 April 1958.

52. "Cal Student Rights Questioned," *The Daily Californian*, vol. 170, no. 30, p. 1, 7 March 1959.

53. B. Stricklin, "Stricklin Requests Chancellor Action," *The Daily Californian*, vol. 170, no. 30, p. 1, 3 December 1959.

54. "Off-Campus Political Activity Considered Legal for Slate," *The Daily Californian*, vol. 170, no. 30, p. 1, 8 April 1959.

55. "Armor, Lubbock in Presidential Finals," *The Daily Californian*, vol. 170, p. 1, 13 May 1959.

56. "Armor Wins -- Closest Vote Ever," *The Daily Californian*, vol. 170, no. 68, p. 1, 1959.

57. "Slate Raps Latest Issues," *The Daily Californian*, vol. 171, no. 56, p. 8, 1959.

58. "Slate Finds Support, Suspicion On Tour," vol. 171, no. 46, p. 1, 17 November 1959.

59. "Berkeley, Battle of the Park," *San Francisco Chronicle*, p. 142, 25 May 1969.

60. "Wide Protest of Guard," *San Francisco Chronicle*, p. 4, 24 May 1969.

61. B. Hamilton, "Instruction to Shot Putters," in *The Worlds of Brutus Hamilton*, Los Angeles, Tafnews, 1975.

62. "Hamilton is not Disappointed Despite Losses and Hurts," *The Daily Californian*, p. Sports Section, 30 March 1960.

63. D. Downey, "Get Well, Big Toe," *San Francisco Chronicle*, p. 27, 12 March 1960.

64. B. Brachman, "Cal Picked in Track – Yerman Ailing," *San Francisco Examiner*, p. 39, 23 April 1960.

65. "NCAA Trials Summary," *San Francisco Chronicle*, p. 27, 18 June 1960.

66. D. Wilson, "NCAA Track Handicap," *San Francisco Chronicle*, p. 27, 18 June 1960.

67. "NCAA Track Summary," *San Francisco Chronicle*, p. 31, 19 June 1960.

68. R. Bergman, "Slight Summer Guide to Bay Area Athletics," *The Daily Californian,* p. Sports Section, 22 June 1960.

69. "Yerman's 46.3 Wins 400-Meter," *San Francisco Chronicle - Sporting Green*, p. 17, 3 July 1960.

70. W. Willis, "California Stars Credit Success to Their Coach," *Oakland Tribune,* p. 20, 3 July 1960.

71. B. Wong, "Greatest Show on Earth Unfolds," *The Daily Californian,* p. 4, 4 July 1960.

72. D. Bloom, *Confessions of a Sportswirter*, New York: Vantage Press Inc., 1988

73. "Life and Love in Olympics," *San Francisco Chronicle*, p. 19, 3 July 1960.

74. M. Durslag, "From First Sports Page," *San Francisco Examiner,* 3 July 1960.

75. W. Adams, "Yerman is Upset Victor in 400," *Sacramento Bee,* pp. D-1, 3 July 1960.

76. UPI, "U.S. Fields Strongest, Zaniest Olympic Team," *Progress-Bulletin,* p. 1, 23 July 1960.

77. G.M. Walton, Beyond Winning; The Timeless Wisdom of Great Philosopher Coaches., Champaign: Leisure Press, 1992.

78. D. Bloom, "Don Bloom's Scoreboard," *Woodland Daily Democrat,* p. 9, 20 Aug 1960.

79. D. Bloom, Confessions of a Sportswirter, New York: Vantage Press Inc., 1988.

80. J. Kieran and A. Daley, the Story ofthe Olumpic Games, 776 B.C. to 1960 AD, Philadelphia: J.B. Lippincott, 1961.

81. J. Kieran and A. Daley.

82. UPI, "87 Nations to Compete," *Los Angeles Examiner,* p. 1, 14 August 1960.

83. J. Kieran and A. Daley.

84. UPI, "Anbulance Crew Eager For Work," *Los Angeles Times,* p. V2, 12 September 1960.

85. M. B. Roberts, "Rudolf Ran and the World Went Wild," [Online]. Available: http://www.espn.com/sportscentury/features/00016444.html. [Accessed 23 May 2021].

86. J. Kieran and A. Daley.

87. New York Times, "Ethiopia Establishes Tradition in Men's Marathons," 1 October 2000. [Online]. Available: http://www.nytimes.com/2000/10/01/olympics/02MARATHON.html. Accessed 30 May 2021].

88. Dibaba, A. T., "The Folklore of Identity Theft: Restoring Abebe Bikila," [Online]. Available: https://advocacy4oromia.org/article/the-folklore-of-identity-theft-restorying-abebe-biqila/. [Accessed 25 July 2021].

89. AP, "American Trackmen 'Choked Up' Say Russians.," *Los Angeles Times,* pp. IV 1-2, 5 September 1960.

90. AP, "Ray Lost Weight Too," *Bakersfield Californian,* p. 11, 23 September 1960.

91. AP, "Ray Lost Weight Too."

92. W. Grimsley, U.S. Stars Told: Keep Out of Bars, " *San Francisco Chronicle*, p.33, 6, September 1960.

93. C. Tonelli, "Seibert, Yerman: View on the Olympics," *The Daily Californian,* 23 September 1960.

94. D. Bloom, *Confessions of a Sportswirter*, New York: Vantage Press Inc., 1988.

95. D. Bloom, *Confessions of a Sportswirter.*

96. D. Bloom, *Confessions of a Sportswirter.*

97. "Athletics at the 1960 Summer Olympics – Men's 400 meters," Wikipedia. n.d. [Online]. Available: https://en.wikipedia.org/wiki/Athletics_at_the_1960_Summer_Olympics_%E2%80%93_Men%27s_400_metres. [Accessed 17 October 2021].

98. D. Bloom, *Confessions of a Sportswirter.*

99. UPI, "Games Failures Spark 'Crash Program'," *The Bakersfield Californian,* p. 31, 12 September 1960.

100. G.M. Walton.

101. Jack and Margo Yerman Collection.

102. D. Bloom, "Olympic Champion Yerman Feted During Homecoming," *Woodland Daily Democrat,* p. 1, 21 October 1960.

103. D. Bloom, "325 Cheer Yerman at CC Luncheon," *Woodland Daily Democrat,* p. 1, 22 October 1960.

104. B. Hamilton, "Dear Friends and Gentle Hearts: London August 5, 1952," in *The Worlds of Brutus Hamilton*, Los Angeles, Tafnews, 1975.

105. Jack and Margo Yerman Collection.

106. Jack and Margo Yerman Collection.

107. Moroni 10:4, *The Book of Mormon, The Church of Jesus Christ of Latter-day Saints*. n.d. [Online]. Available: https://www.churchofjesuschrist.org/study/scriptures/bofm/moro/10?lang=eng. [Accessed 22 August 2021].

108. D. Gitlin, "5 More Firsts Give CISM Track Win," *Stars and Stripes,* p. 22C, 7 August 1962.

109. Wikipedia, "Men's 400 metres world record progression," n.d. [Online]. Available: https://en.wikipedia.org/wiki/Men%27s_400_metres_world_record_progression. [Accessed 23 May 2021].

110. "Foriegn News Briefs," *The Register,* p. 6A, 9 August 1962.

111. H. Scott, "Soviet General At Heidelberg," *Stars and Stripes,* vol. 21, no. 113, p. 2, 9 August 1962.

112. H. Scott.

113. D. Bloom, "Jack Runs for Russians at Heidelberg," *Woodland Daily Democrat,* p. Sports Section, n.d.

114. F. Landis, "How was [it] like to make an international phone call in the 60s," n.d. [Online]. Available: https://www.quora.com/How-was-like-to-make-an-international-phone-call-in-the-60s. [Accessed 23 May 2021].

115. R.J. Chapius and A. E. Joel, 100 Years of Telephone Switching, Part 1, Clifton, PA: IOS Press, 2003, p. 290.

116. B. Hamilton, "To Mr. and Mrs. Jack Yerman; November 16, 1962," in *The Worlds of Brutus Hamilton*, Tafnews, 1975.

117. Jack and Margo Yerman Collection.

118. Jack and Margo Yerman Collection.

119. Jack and Margo Yerman Collection.

120. "A Roundup of the Sports Information of the Week," *Sports Illustrated,* 4 March 1963.

121. B. Hamilton, "To Jim, Bob, Col. Frank and Jess: December 1, 1955," in *The Worlds of Brutus Hamilton*, Los Angeles, Tafnews, 1975.

122. [Company Name Omited], "Swiftest Man In A Business Suit," *Quarterly Magazine,* pp. 3-4, 1963.

123. R. Eveleth, "Forty Years Ago, Women Had a Hard Time Getting Credit Cards," smithsonian.com, 8 January 2014. [Online]. Available: https://www.smithsonian-mag.com/smart-news/forty-years-ago-women-had-a-hard-time-getting-credit-cards-180949289/. [Accessed 6 June 2021].

124. J. Hill, "Fact check: Post detailing 9 things women couldn't do before 1971 is mostly right." USA Today, 28 October 2020 [Online]. Available: https://www.usatoday.com/story/news/factcheck/2020/10/28/fact-check-9-things-women-couldnt-do-1971-mostly-right/3677101001/. [Access August 2021]

125. G.M. Walton.

126. "Brown's 6-11 High Jump Sets Mark," *Oakland Tribune,* 1 March 1964.

127. "Youth Village Dominates Track Meet," *Oakland Tribune,* 15 March 1964.

128. "Adolph Plummer," 20 October 2020. [Online]. Available: https://en.wikipedia.org/wiki/Adolph_Plummer. [Accessed July 2021].

129. "Woodland's Jack Yerman Awaits Boat to Olympics," *Sacramento Bee,* 10 July 1960.

130. "Yerman Eyes 1968 Olympic Games," *Oakland Tribune*, p. E-59, 11 February, 1965.

131. C. Grieve, "Newest Thing in Track: 'Citius 4' by Bowden," *The San Francisco Examiner,* p. 43, 13 February 1965.

132. Philadelphia Inquirer, p. 28, 22 February 1965.

133. E. Bericht, "Terror gegen Berlin soll noch bis Sonntag forgestzt werden," *Berliner Morgenpost,* sec. A, 1., 9 April 1965.

134. "Larrabee Sets 400-Meter Dash Record," *The Times-News Sports,* 9 April 1965.

135. B. Hamilton, "Prayer From Patiala," in *The Worlds of Brutus Hamilton*, Los Angeles, Tafnews, 1975.

136. J. Dickerson, "Teamsters, GOP, Forged Increasingly Close Links," *The Washington Post*, 25 July 1985 [Online]. Available: https://www.washingtonpost.com/archive/politics/1985/07/25/teamsters-gop-forged-increasingly-close-links/87eee847-76f3-45cf-b64b-3a783c5f3503/. [Accessed September 2021].

137. Jack and Margo Yerman Collection.

138. B. Hamilton, "To Mr. Avery Brundage: November 28, 1953," in *The Worlds of Brutus Hamilton*, Los Angeles, Tafnews, 1975.

139. S. Sharf, "New York and Florida Dominate 2016 List of America's Most Expensive ZIP Codes," 12 August 2016. [Online]. Available: https://www.forbes.com/sites/samanthasharf/2016/12/08/new-york-and-florida-dominate-2016-list-of-americas-most-expensive-zip-codes/?sh=a0d5f1c48599. [Accessed 24 May 2021].

140. Jack and Margo Yerman Collection.

141. B. D. McKnight, "We Fight for Peace: Twenty-three American Soldiers, Prisoners of War, and Turncoats in the Korean War," Kent State University Press, May 2016. [Online]. Available: https://www.h-net.org/reviews/showpdf.php?id=42834. [Accessed 24 May 2021].

142. Jack and Margo Yerman Collection.

143. R. Jones, "Forward," in *The Wave*, Laurel-Leaf Books, 1981.

144. Jack and Margo Yerman Collection.

145. Jack and Margo Yerman Collection.

146. B. Hamilton, "To Mr. Frank Storment: February 4, 1958," in *The Worlds of Brutus Hamilton*, Los Angeles, Tafnews, 1975.

147. "Dow Jones - DJIA - 100 Year Historical Chart," *Macrotrends*, [Online]. Available: https://www.macrotrends.net/1319/dow-jones-100-year-historical-chart. [Accessed 24 May 2021].

148. AP, "Zambian Copper Shipment To Be Cut," *The Herald World of Business,* p. 18, 2 February 1967.

149. "Zambian Copper Output Restored to Normal," *St. Lois Post Dispatch,* 12 June 1967.

150. "Rhodesian Train Carries Copper," *The Baltimore Sun,* 1 Jun 1966.

151. "Powerful Zambesi Provides Magnificence of Victoria Falls," *Clarion Ledgeer,* 19 April 1967.

152. "Production Up," *Cincinnati Enquirer,* 27 February 1967.

153. "President of Zambia Faces Impossible Job," *The Los Angeles Times,* 12 May 1966.

154. Reuters, "Zambia's First Lady Frowns on Mini-Skirt," *The Gazetter,* 26 April 1967.

155. "Operation Rolling Thunder," 5 March 2015. [Online]. Available: https://www.historylearningsite.co.uk/vietnam-war/operation-rolling-thunder/. [Accessed 24 May 2021].

156. Blitzkerieg - Israeli Style," *Daily News,* 7 June 1967.

157. "No Right to Close Suez, Says Wilson. Arab Mobs Burn U.S., British Consulates. Newsmen, Including 2 Americans, Die in Mideast," *The Tampa Tribune,* 7 June 1967.

158. B. Hamilton, "Prayer From Patiala."

159. H. Editors, "Senator McCarthy says communists are in State Department," A&E Television Networks, 2021 February 2021. [Online]. Available: https://www.history.com/this-day-in-history/mccarthy-says-communists-are-in-state-department. [Accessed 30 May 2021].

160. Oshinksky, "Fact from Fiction: Joseph McCarthy the Tail Gunner," Spring 2020. [Online]. Available: https://articles.historynet.com/fact-from-fiction-joseph-mccarthy-the-tail-gunner.htm. [Accessed 20 06 2021].

161. Oshinksky.

162. "Devinitions.net," n.d. [Online]. Available: https://www.definitions.net/definition/mccarthyism. [Accessed 2021 30 May].

163. Life Magazine , "Hell Breaks Loose in Paradise," *Life,* vol. 54, no. 17, pp. 73-84, 26 April 1963.

164. United Press International, "J. Edgar Hoover: Black Panther Greatest Threat to U.S. Security," UPI, 16 July 1969. [Online]. Available: https://www.upi.com/Archives/1969/07/16/J-Edgar-Hoover-Black-Panther-Greatest-Threat-to-US-Security/1571551977068/. [Accessed 20 June 2021].

165. Superior California News, Liable Action Names Papers Owners, *Sacramento Bee,* 30 March 1972.

166. B. Hamilton, "Prayer From Patiala."

167. Political Advertisement, "What's Wrong With Civil Rights," *Oakland Tribune,* p. 28-C, 22, Aug. 1975.

168. B. Lyman, "'Stand up for America' – George Wallace's chaotic, prophetic campaign," 20 August 2018. [Online]. Available: https://www.usatoday.com/story/news/nation-now/1968-project/2018/08/16/stand-up-america-george-wallaces-chaotic-prophetic-campaign/961043002/. [Accessed October 2020].

169. D. Davis, "Olympic Athletes Who Took a Stand," August 2008. [Online]. Available: http://www.smithsonianmag.com/people-places/indelible-olympics-200808.html. [Accessed October 2020].

170. "Tommie Smith," Spartacus Educational, n.d. [Online]. Available: https://sparta-cus-educational.com/CRsmithT.htm. [Accessed 24 May 2021].

171. B. Snider-McGrath, "Peter Norman: unsung hero of the 1968 Olympic protest," Canadian Running Magazine, 16 June 1920. [Online]. Available: https://running-magazine.ca/the-scene/the-third-man-who-protested-on-the-1968-olympic-200m-podium/. [Accessed 24 May 2021].

172. J. Montegue, "The third man: The forgotten Black Power Hero," 25 April 2012. [Online]. Available: https://www.cnn.com/2012/04/24/sport/olympics-norman-black-power/index.html. [Accessed 14 May 2021].

173. "Committe to Analyze Graduation Nees Is Being Organized Here," *Chico Enterprise Record,* 30 Jan 1970.

174. L. Steinberg, "Chico High Symposium: Bircher Tells Gathering Students Easiest Marks for Communist Influence," *Chico Enterprise Record,* 21 April 1967.

175. "Editor: Register," *The Napa Valley Register,* 21 March 1967.

176. *Caduceus,* Chico High School Yearbook, Vol. LXV, p. 122.

177. G. Traynham, "Gary's Guff," *Woodland Daily Democrat*, p. 14, 3 January 1968.

178. P. McCarthy, "Top Track Stars Open Indoor Season," *Oakland Tribune,* 7 January 1967.

179. S. Baillie, "Yerman Rough But Not Dirty," *Los Angeles Times,* 9 February 1967.

180. "Student Point of View, 'Generally Felt It was Worth It'," *Chico Enterprise Record,* 7 February 1969.

181. M. Erickson, "Black Olympic Track Star Stresses Education Needs," *Chico Enterprise Record,* 6 February 1969.

182. J. Burrell, "Talk by Black Bower Sprinter Protested," Letters to the *Editor, Chico Enterprise Record,"* 5 February 1969.

183. H.G. Ruffin II, "Tommie Smith," Blackpast.org, 21 April 2011. [Online]. Available: https://www.blackpast.org/african-american-history/smith-tommie-1944/#:~:tex-t=Tommie%20Smith%20is%20best%20known,family%20worked%20as%20field%20laborers. [Accessed 30 May 2021].

184. N. Tower, "Olympic Project for Human Rights lit fire for 1968 protests," Arizona State University, 8 October 2018. [Online]. Available: https://globalsportmatters.com/mexico/2018/10/08/olympic-project-for-human-rights-lit-fire-for-1968-pro-tests/. [Accessed 30 May 2021].

185. "Student Point of View, 'Generally Felt It was Worth It.'"

186. "Bill Berry, Junior," *Chico Enterprise Record,* 25 October 1968.

187. M. Erickson.

188. S. Alois. Personal Interview. 28 August 2021.

189. M. Erickson, "Black Olympic Track Star Stresses Education Needs," *Chico Enterprise Record,* 6 February 1969.

190. M. Erickson.

191. "Student Point of View, 'Generally Felt It was Worth It.'"

192. "Student Point of View."

193. M. Shapiro, "How Tommie Smith's 'Cry for Freedom' Sparked a Legacy of Athlete Acivism," ABG-SI LLC. Sports Illustrated, 12 August 2020. [Online]. Available: https://www.si.com/olympics/2020/08/12/tommie-smith-john-carlos-1968-olympics-protest-athlete-activism. [Accessed 30 May 2021].

194. M. Erickson.

195. M. Erickson.

196. G.M. Walton.

197. Lost Duchman Chapter 5917 Arizona, "A Short History Of E Clampus Vitus," Skunks' Misery Redux, n.d. [Online]. Available: http://www.ecv5917.com/Articles/ecvhistory.html. [Accessed 1 June 2021].

198. "From the Mines," *New York Tribune,* 16 March 1853.

199. J. McKinley, "Promoting Offbeat History Between the Drinks," The New York Times, 13 October 2008. [Online]. Available: https://www.nytimes.com/2008/10/14/us/14california.html. [Accessed 30 May 2021].

200. A. Barnes, "Interesting Donkey Facts," habitatforhorses.org, n.d. [Online]. Available: https://www.habitatforhorses.org/interesting-donkey-facts/. [Accessed May 2021].

201. Record Derby Crowd," *Paradise Post,* 1 May 1970.

202. Record Derby Crowd.

203. "Yerman Entry Wins Derby," *Paradise Post,* p. 2, 30 April 1971.

204. "Yerman Entry Wins Derby."

205. B. Hamilton, "To Mr. and Mrs. Jack Yerman; November 16, 1962," in *The Worlds of Brutus Hamilton*, Tafnews, 1975.

206. "Social Events," *The Marysville Appeal,* 1 August 1925.

207. R. Yonash, The Weimar Joint Sanatorium and the Weimar Cemetery, Colfax: Colfax Area Historical Society, 2012.

208. "Henry Flamme of Tudor Dies At the Weimar Hospital," *The Sutter County Farmer,* December 17, 1926

209. "Wilson," *Appeal Democrat,* 14 August 1931.

210. "Lloyd [sic]Yerman Hurt When Horse Falls," *Woodland Daily Democrat,* 25 July 1932.

211. "Ask Police to Locate Three Missing in 3 Places," *The Bulletin,* 23 June 1922.

212. "Yuba City Girl Weds Lloyd [sic] C. Yerman," *Woodland Daily Democrat,* 16 November 1935.

213. E. Blakemore, "Why Many Married Women Were Banned from Working During the Great Depression," 21 July 2019. [Online]. Available: https://www.history.com/news/great-depression-married-women-employment. [Accessed 30 May 2021].

214. Five Married Nurses Still At County Hospital to be Replaced By Single Girls," *Sacramento Bee,* 16 June 1933.

215. "Man Injured When Horse Stumbles, Falls," *Woodland Democrat,* p. 1, 4 January 1936.

216. "Wilson," *Appeal Democrat,* 4 February 1936.

217. "Town Give Free Camping To Tourists," *The San Francisco Examiner,* 17 June 1917.

218. N. Rego, "Days Gone By Liquor Goes Back On Sale In California in 1934 When Prohibition Ends," *The Mercury News,* 8 January 2014.

219. "Driver Fined on Drunken Charge," *Oroville Mercury Register,* 7 April 1938.

220. "Loyd C. Yerman Fractures Wrist," *Oroville Mercury Register,* 29 June 1938.

221. "Needy Will Go Hungry Unless More Funds Given For Relief," *Oroville Mercury Register,* 18 March 1933.

222. "Reports Jacket Stolen," *Oroville Mercury Register,* 9 December 1938.

223. H. Zoto, "SHOCK: Widely feared ad misunderstood, electroconvulsive therapy is really a safe and painless 'medical miracle of our time,'" *San Francisco Examiner,* 25 September 1960.

224. M. Zellerbaack, "Electroschock: Miracle, Menace?," *San Francsco Examiner,* 23 October 1960.

225. B. Hamilton, "Prayer From Patiala."

226. "These Folks Said Merry Christmas," *Press Democrat,* 8 December 1957.

227. "Town, Country of Woodland Plans Show," *Sacramento Bee*, 6 February 1954.

228. G.M. Walton.

229. G. Williams, "Quiet Pride," *Paradise Post,* Sports Sec, C. 2, 15 June 1984.

230. G. Williams.

231. U.S. Department of State, "The Olympic Boycott, 1980," Information released online from January 20, 2001 to January 20, 2009. [Online]. Available: https://2001-2009.state.gov/r/pa/ho/time/qfp/104481.htm#:~:text=In%201980%2C%20the%20United%20States,countries%20sent%20athletes%20to%20compete. [Accessed 27 May 2021].

232. G. Williams.

233. W. Willis, "California Stars Credit Success to Their Coach," *Oakland Tribune,* p. 20, 3 July 1960.

234. B. Hamilton, "Darling Jeanie [The Hamilton's Daughter]," in *The Worlds of Brutus Hamilton*, Los Angleles, Tafpress, 1975.